SEPTEMBER
SONGS

SEPTEMBER SONGS

THE GOOD NEWS ABOUT MARRIAGE
IN THE LATER YEARS

MAGGIE SCARF

RIVERHEAD BOOKS

a member of Penguin Group (USA) Inc.

New York

2008

R

RIVERHEAD BOOKS
Published by the Penguin Group
Penguin Group (USA) Inc., 375 Hudson Street, New York, New York 10014, USA • Penguin Group
(Canada), 90 Eglinton Avenue East, Suite 700, Toronto, Ontario M4P 2Y3, Canada (a division of
Pearson Canada Inc.) • Penguin Books Ltd, 80 Strand, London WC2R 0RL, England • Penguin Ireland,
25 St Stephen's Green, Dublin 2, Ireland (a division of Penguin Books Ltd) • Penguin Group (Australia),
250 Camberwell Road, Camberwell, Victoria 3124, Australia (a division of Pearson Australia Group
Pty Ltd) • Penguin Books India Pvt Ltd, 11 Community Centre, Panchsheel Park, New Delhi–110 017,
India • Penguin Group (NZ), 67 Apollo Drive, Rosedale, North Shore 0632, New Zealand (a division
of Pearson New Zealand Ltd) • Penguin Books (South Africa) (Pty) Ltd, 24 Sturdee Avenue, Rosebank,
Johannesburg 2196, South Africa

Penguin Books Ltd, Registered Offices:
80 Strand, London WC2R 0RL, England

Copyright © 2008 by Maggie Scarf

Grateful acknowledgment is made to reprint the following:
"September Song"
From the musical production *Knickerbocker Holiday*
Words by Maxwell Anderson; Music by Kurt Weill
TRO-© 1938 (Renewed) Hampshire House Publishing Corp.,
New York and Warner Chappell Music, Inc., Los Angeles, CA. Used by permission.

Library of Congress Cataloging-in-Publication Data

Scarf, Maggie, date.
September songs : the good news about marriage in the later years / Maggie Scarf.
p.   cm.
ISBN 978-1-59448-850-4
1. Marriage.   2. Older people—psychology.   3. Love in old age.   I. Title.
HQ734.S37645   2008   2008025187
306.81—dc22

Printed in the United States of America
1   3   5   7   9   10   8   6   4   2

Book design by Chris Welch

FOR HERB, ALWAYS

CONTENTS

Preface 1

One. LYNN AND CARL MCBRIDE 25
A GIFT OF TIME

Two. DOES DIVORCE MAKE PEOPLE HAPPY? 45

Three. LIZ AND JEFF DENNISON 69
CLASSMATES

Four. TAKING TIME SERIOUSLY 87

Five. JEAN AND NED DONALDSON 105
THE SIMPLE LIFE

Six. JACKIE AND STEVE WINSTON (1) 131
TRANSITIONING: A FOOT IN EACH WORLD

Seven. JACKIE AND STEVE WINSTON (2) 159
RETIREMENT MYTHS, RETIREMENT REALITIES

Eight. CLAUDIA AND DOUGLAS HAMILTON 178
AN UNCERTAIN FUTURE

Nine. NANCY AND DAVID STERNBERG 210
IN SICKNESS AND IN HEALTH

Epilogue 229
Acknowledgments 241
Selected References 245
Index 251

AUTHOR'S NOTE

The couples whose interviews have been used in these pages have agreed to let their stories be told, with minor changes as far as identifying details are concerned (names, professions, names of family members, geographical location in some instances, etc.). The life narratives described here are therefore factual, aside from the omission or change of such unnecessarily specific information.

The best is yet to be,
The last of life, for which the first was made. . . .

—ROBERT BROWNING

SEPTEMBER
SONGS

n the course of the twentieth century something akin to a miracle has occurred: in this brief span of evolutionary time, thirty years of life have been added to normal human life expectancy. For the first time in the history of our species, the majority of people born in the Western world can now expect to survive into old age. As social scientists Laura Carstensen and Susan Charles have noted in an important paper entitled "Taking Time Seriously," "The enormity of this advance is unprecedented. A new stage has been added to the life-cycle."

These "bonus" years of life have been bequeathed to us not only by the dazzling array of medical advances achieved in the mid-twentieth century, such as the Salk vaccine, antibiotics, etc. Less glamorous (and therefore less trumpeted) has been the fact that this bequest of added years has resulted from the introduction of sewers and improved sanitation, which in turn suppressed waterborne diseases such as typhoid fever and dysentery. These and a myriad of other developments have served to change the natural course of the life span, adding more years to the average person's lifetime than had been gained during the previous millennia of human history.

A glance at the mortality statistics that existed at the outset of the twentieth century will quickly underline this point. These figures reveal that the average person's life expectancy at that time was a brief 49.2 years. Indeed, *half* of all children born in the early 1900s would perish before they reached the age of five, largely due to infectious diseases such as diphtheria, influenza, infectious diarrhea and the host of other illnesses that preyed upon the very young.

This stark child-mortality statistic stands in bold contrast to the fate of children born later in the century, who would not only survive the vulnerable early years of life but would live on into the ripe years of mature adulthood. By the end of the twentieth century, the average man's life expectancy at birth was 73.6 years, and the average woman's life expectancy at birth was 79.4 years. These numbers averaged out at 76.5 years for both sexes in the year 1997 (and that figure has been climbing slowly ever since). In what might be seen as the twinkle of a historical eye, the human life span had become almost three decades longer.

LIFE EXPECTANCY BY AGE-GROUP AND SEX, IN YEARS, 1900–1997

	1900	1910	1920	1930	1940	1950	1960	1970	1980	1990	1997
Life Expectancy at Birth											
Total	49.2	51.5	56.4	59.2	63.6	68.1	69.9	70.8	73.9	75.4	76.5
Men	47.9	49.9	55.5	57.7	61.6	65.5	66.8	67	70.1	71.8	73.6
Women	50.7	53.2	57.4	60.9	65.9	71	73.2	74.6	77.6	78.8	79.4

	1900	1910	1920	1930	1940	1950	1960	1970	1980	1990	1997
Life Expectancy at Age 65											
Total	11.9	11.6	12.5	12.2	12.8	13.8	14.4	15	16.5	17.3	17.7
Men	11.5	11.2	12.2	11.7	12.1	12.7	13	13	14.2	15.1	15.9
Women	12.2	12	12.7	12.8	13.6	15	15.8	16.8	18.4	19	19.2
Life Expectancy at Age 85											
Total	4	4	4.2	4.2	4.3	4.7	4.6	5.3	6	6.2	6.3
Men	3.8	3.9	4.1	4	4.1	4.4	4.4	4.7	5.1	5.3	5.5
Women	4.1	4.1	4.3	4.3	4.5	4.9	4.7	5.6	6.4	6.7	6.6

LIFE EXPECTANCY BY AGE-GROUP AND RACE, IN YEARS, 1997

	White	Black
Life Expectancy at Birth	77.1	71.1
Life Expectancy at Age 65	17.8	16.1
Life Expectancy at Age 85	6.2	6.4

Reference population: These data refer to the resident population.

Source: National Vital Statistics System.

THE NOON OF LIFE?

In the year 1931 the great Swiss psychologist Carl Jung wrote: "The age of forty is the noon of life." During that midlife period, he stated, we are in possession of our full adult powers, but each of us is conscious that our personal sun is entering a new meridian. "We cannot live the afternoon of life according to life's morning. . . . [F]or what was great in the morning will be little at evening, and what was true in the morning will at evening have become a lie."

Much as I can appreciate the beauty of this statement, it is sadly out-of-date in the early part of the twenty-first century. At the present time, our ideas about what is "middle adulthood" are far more fluid. A recent U.S. Census Bureau report states that many people now in their early sixties, when queried about what stage of life they are currently in, will say that *they* are in the midlife period. To be sure, given the phenomenal changes that have occurred in human life expectancy, what is meant by "middle age" may now be being stretched out like the saltwater taffy that, as a little girl, I used to buy on the Atlantic City boardwalk.

Shall we call this added phase of life "midlife-plus" or "later adulthood"? The very question makes me think of a quote from a sixty-six-year-old woman I interviewed for my work on couples over fifty (see chapter 9). She is someone I'd talked with twenty years earlier for my book on marriage, *Intimate Partners*. The intervening years have touched her lightly, for I found her to be as trim and pretty as she had been those many years earlier.

Here is what she said, at age sixty-six, about the whole idea of being "elderly." "When you read an article that says: 'Elderly seventy-year-old man swerves off the road,' or 'Elderly woman of sixty-five held up in parking lot,' I say to myself, 'Oh my God! That's not *my* definition of 'elderly.' Okay, the years between fifty-six and sixty-six are now gone—they went like smoke in the wind. So my definition of 'elderly' is now seventy-six instead of sixty-six. And it's going to advance the further along I get." She laughed. "That's not to say I would like to go back and relive the early years, but that maybe I would like to have *ten years* of being sixty-six. And maybe *ten years* of being sixty-seven and *ten years* of being sixty-eight. . . . I just wish there were some way of slowing the clock down."

A couple of decades earlier, during the time of our first set of interviews, this woman and her husband had been dealing with some significant marital and family problems. But now some twenty years had gone by, and I found both members of the pair to be much more relaxed and contented with each other, even serene. They, like a number of over-fifty couples I interviewed in the course of my research, were finding these older adult years to be a very *good* time of their lives. This was not what I'd expected when I began my research on this relatively unexplored stage of the life cycle; and, like Dorothy in *The Wizard of Oz*, I felt myself being whirled around and around for a while until I touched down in a whole new place, a world that was full of zest, ardor and surprises.

SEPTEMBER SONG

It was the fall term of 2005, and I was standing in the lecture room of Yale University's Whitney Humanities Center, where I was a visiting fellow for the academic year. With me was the well-known composer Martin Bresnick, who was peppering me with a fusillade of intelligent, incisive questions about the project on "couples over fifty" in which I was involved: *Were any of the partners remarried people? What led them to become volunteers? How did I know they were telling me the truth? What were my findings thus far?*

I'll admit to having felt somewhat flustered, because a number of Bresnick's questions were ones that couldn't be answered in sound bites. I explained that it was still early days for me, but I was carrying out a series of intensive interviews with over-fifty volunteers who had come to me from a variety of sources—for example, some came from audiences in lectures I had given, and others were couples I had interviewed at length twenty years earlier, in the course of work I was doing at that time. Still others were people who had heard by word of mouth about the research I was doing, or had learned of it from a scattering of posters put up in churches, temples and libraries. As for what I had discovered thus far—there I hesitated, then said that these conversations were turning out to be much different from anything I had anticipated. The marital partners I was interviewing (including some pairs who'd been very troubled when I talked with them a number of years ago) seemed to be doing awfully well, far better than I might have predicted. Actually, I was feeling somewhat confounded by my findings at the moment.

When Martin Bresnick made no comment, I heard myself rattling on. I explained that, given the remarkable extension of the life span, many gerontologists now make a distinction between two groups of people in older adulthood. One group is the "young-old" cohort, which is the large group of individuals between fifty and seventy-five years of age. "This is the one I am focusing on," I explained. The second group are those in the "old-old" cohort; that is, people in the seventy-five-and-older age bracket.

"There's a huge amount of research on the old-old cohort, particularly the frail elderly," I continued. "The same is true of people in their middle years, say thirty-five to fifty, for there's been so much interest in the so-called midlife crisis." I shrugged, adding that the "young-old" group I was studying (fifty to seventy-five)—which now included the leading edge of the baby boom—hadn't yet received anywhere near the same degree of research attention.

At that moment, I realized that Bresnick was smiling and humming something softly, under his breath. It was a melody that was faintly familiar. I stopped speaking, then asked him what was that song he was humming.

Bresnick told me it was music that had been composed by Kurt Weill for the Broadway show *Knickerbocker Holiday*, back in the 1930s. Then he began quietly singing some of the lyrics.

Oh, it's a long long while
from May to December,
but the days grow short, when you reach September. . . .

He paused, said he couldn't recall the next verse, but kept humming, *dum-de-dum*, as if waiting for it to spring into his mind. There was another extended pause while a group of colleagues walked around us on both sides, glancing at us curiously. I looked at the composer, silently imploring him to remember more of the lyrics. . . . And after a moment, he held up a finger as if to say, "Some of it's coming back to me." Then he continued:

Oh, the days dwindle down
To a precious few,
September, November!
And these few precious days . . .
I'll spend with you,
These precious days
I'll spend with you.

"That's lovely," I said, touched by this melody, those words. "What is the name of that song?"

"It's called 'September Song,'" Martin Bresnick replied.

"Well, if you want to know what my book is about, that's it," I said.

THE AGE PYRAMID

In a metaphorical sense, this was true, but in a more literal one, my response was not statistically accurate. When "September Song" was composed, in the late thirties, a male's life expectancy was just under 61.6 years in the United States, while a female's hovered around age sixty-six. So, if our lovers in the song were in their late thirties or early forties in 1938—that is, born around the turn of the century, or earlier—their time remaining was indeed as precious and brief as the lyrics of "September Song" suggest.

By the time the end of the twentieth century had rolled around, however, life expectancy at birth—shown here in graphic form—had increased to 73.6 for males and 79.4 for females. Moreover, a male who reached age sixty-five in 1997 could expect to live another 15.9 years, while a female could expect to live another 19.2 years. As these figures suggest, what Jung termed "the afternoon of life" had grown considerably longer. Rather than consisting of "these few precious days," it could stretch to some three decades beyond the age of fifty.

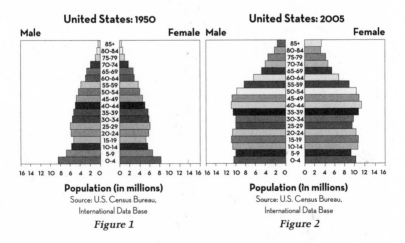

United States: 1950

Male   Female

Population (in millions)
Source: U.S. Census Bureau,
International Data Base

Figure 1

United States: 2005

Male   Female

Population (in millions)
Source: U.S. Census Bureau,
International Data Base

Figure 2

At the present time, a large number of older adults—those in their fifties, sixties, early seventies—have emerged in the human life span in industrialized, developed countries such as our own (and there are indications that the developing countries are catching up with us). Especially given the falling birthrate worldwide, we are now living in an aging world—a fact that can be demonstrated by a quick perusal of the "age pyramids" shown above and below.

In 1950 (Figure 1), the two bottom lines mark the beginning of the baby boom (ages 0–4 and 5–9). In the next illustration (Figure 2, fifty-five years later), the lines in the middle are the early boomers (now ages 55–59 and 60–64). The lines immediately below (from ages 45–54) represent the decade of the baby boomers in its full flowering, and the youngest of the boomers are in their early forties. This figure depicts the year 2005.

The following display (Figure 3) pictures the population as seen in the year 2025. Now the three lines at the top denote the starting edge of the boomers; the three lines directly below depict the baby boom bulge (people now ages 60–75). In the final box, the trailing edge of the

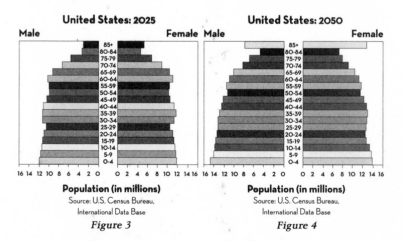

United States: 2025

Male   Female

Population (in millions)
Source: U.S. Census Bureau,
International Data Base

Figure 3

United States: 2050

Male   Female

Population (in millions)
Source: U.S. Census Bureau,
International Data Base

Figure 4

boomers is captured in the top line, those eighty-five and over. This is the year 2050, a hundred years after the outset of the post–World War II population explosion. The most fascinating aspect of these illustrations can be seen in the different numbers of surviving age-eighty-five individuals as you move from the first illustration to the last one. In an increasingly aging world, the "age pyramid" has grown to look less like a conventional pyramid and more like an irregular pyramid with an odd protrusion at its crest.

What these figures demonstrate is that for partners over fifty, a new stage of adult living—and of couplehood—has materialized. The average pair will live together for a substantial period of time after their children (if there are any) have left home. What can be learned about their experience of this time of adult living, which is effectively neither middle adulthood nor old age and which has received comparatively little notice or attention?

At this point I think it worth noting that a stage of the life cycle we now accept as a given—that is, adolescence—is also of relatively recent vintage. The term was actually first used to designate this developmental phase in a *Popular Science* article published in 1941. In a way, the stage of older adult life (fifty to seventy-five years) that I've been studying seems almost like a bookend to that earlier phase of life-changing flux and transition—a kind of adult-escence, if you will. Like adolescence, adult-escence is a period of living that requires significant changes in a person's basic orientation to the self and to his or her surroundings.

For the overarching tasks of later adolescence have to do with separating from the family of origin, redirecting the intense feelings for the parental love-objects and finding ways of being intimate with a sexual peer. This stage of living also involves the crucial developmental task of forging an individual identity—finding an answer to the question *Who am I?* that feels as if it fits right and is comfortable.

The developmental trajectory of the older adult couple is almost a parallel version of the process just described. For once again, *intimacy* becomes a dominant priority: the marital partners must now move closer and become more intimate as mates rather than focusing on their careers or their departing or departed offspring. In a real sense, husband and wife must *refind* each other. Moreover, since they are perched on the edge of the retirement years, both must once again confront identity issues and get to work on fashioning a changed self-definition. The basic question being posed is eerily familiar, though somewhat different this time around. It is: *Who am I, once I have left my parenting and/or occupational roles behind me?*

Nevertheless, it must be said that while most adolescents experience and create a lot of turmoil during the passage from childhood into independent adulthood, a great many older adults seem to look forward to their later, retirement years without much consternation. In fact, the average age at which Americans choose to leave the workplace has actually fallen: it is currently sixty to sixty-two years old. This means that retirement itself has retreated from the once-standard age sixty-five; however, many social scientists believe it is likely to rise again in the near future. This is because the age at which Social Security benefits kick in was recently moved up to sixty-seven years.

Of course, there are many situations in which the decision to retire is *not* made on the basis of financial concerns alone. Indeed there are many instances in which this life choice is inherently entangled with how much of an individual's personal identity is invested in a particular job or profession. Some people choose to leave the workplace at the first feasible opportunity—the time when they feel they'll have enough resources to live on—while others cling to their work role until the last possible moment. The individuals in the latter group are those who feel that their career identity is indistinguishable from who they are as human beings. The question "Who am I in the absence of this career?" is one they are unable to answer.

THE PARADOX OF AGING

One can readily imagine why the years of later adulthood might be a problematic time of life. We live in a society that lionizes the glories of youth, and is rife with an attendant fear of aging. A brief glance at a rack of Hallmark birthday greeting cards testifies quickly to this state of affairs. For example, the cover of one card, illustrated with two merrily dancing partners, proclaims: "You're 60! You should dance! You should sing! You should celebrate!" But on the inside, the text reads: "You should take an anti-inflammatory of some kind." The "joke," but also the message, is that if you've reached the age of sixty, your health is deteriorating.

Another Hallmark card shows a young woman saying, "Heard you turned 60." The inside text, however, reads, "I said, 'HEARD YOU TURNED 60.' " In other words, if you've reached the age of sixty, you are already hard of hearing. Even a fortieth birthday card bears the opening line: "You're 40 now, so embrace it, Love it, Love It!" Inside, however, it says, "Now sit down. Breathe into a paper bag. Deep breaths. You'll be okay." The relentless communication is always: Aging Is Decay and Decline.

On the front of yet another card is a picture of a smiling, plump, gray-haired woman wearing large sunglasses and clad in a print bathing suit. She is leaning against a fence with a blue sea stretching behind her. Above her is the statement, "If you've got it . . ." But inside, the card reads: "Please, I beg of you, don't do this with it" . . . in other words, don't show it.

The implication or "joke" is that the older, heavyset woman should do the decent thing and make herself invisible. Unless a female is young and comely, she should stay out of sight, for her very presence is a blight upon the landscape.

The widespread cultural beliefs reflected in these crudely "witty" greeting cards are mirrored in an abundant psychological literature on the subject. For example, in a collection of research papers entitled *Ageism*—a book devoted entirely to studies of age discrimination—I came across such patronizing titles as "Doddering but Dear: Process, Content and Function in Stereotyping of Older Persons"; "Ageism: Denying the Face of the Future"; "Implicit Ageism"; and "Acting Your Age."

And yet smack in the middle of one of these negatively toned essays was an unexpected statement to the effect that, yes, such age-related prejudice does exist and is widespread; but at the same time, *older adults seem to be relatively happy.* The consistent, worldwide finding, these particular researchers note, is that the majority of men and women in their fifties, sixties and seventies enjoy a subjective sense of contentment and well-being.

Why should this be so? It is a question to which nobody can supply a definitive answer. But these social scientists dubbed the prevalent good feeling among older adults "the paradox of aging." And in fact this "paradox" is what I have encountered in many of my interviews with fifty-plus couples. It is also what a band of life-cycle developmental researchers have been reporting in a variety of psychological journals. A leader of this group is Professor Laura Carstensen, director of Stanford University's Life-span Development Laboratory as well as founding director of the Center on Longevity at Stanford University.

In a series of papers on psychology and aging, Carstensen and her colleagues have been demonstrating that while there are clearly physical and mental age-associated declines of many sorts, there seems to be *no* demonstrable loss when it comes to emotional processing and emotional control. Older adults not only preserve their capacities in this domain, they often show improvement as they age.

Carstensen and her coworkers have been developing an impressive theory (described in chapter 4) called "socioemotional selectivity." Its core thesis is founded on the notion that older people take time *very seriously* in terms of the years they have left to live—and their motivations and behavior shift accordingly. As a result, in the autumn of their lives, most older adults go about pruning their relationships and arranging matters systematically in ways that will help them avoid potentially negative, hurtful experiences and enhance what Dr. Carstensen calls the "positivity effect"—that is, positive things happening in their lives.

Carstensen's view is that the key to understanding the psychology of the older adult is his/her growing internal awareness of the ticking clock of life. The realization that time is a diminishing resource brings about a heightened emphasis on feelings and emotions—a movement toward social interactions that are meaningful and away from people and events that seem negative, trivial or outright toxic. It is this growing appreciation of life's eventual ending that impels older men and older women to assign high value to emotional intimacy, to seek meaning in life and to establish feelings of embeddedness within a valued, trusted and close community.

I describe Carstensen's work in much more detail later in the book.

But for now, let me simply say that there is no smaller, closer community than that of husband and wife.

MARRIAGE, CIRCA THE TWENTY-FIRST CENTURY

In a time of social flux such as our own, a relevant question is: What proportion of the population actually makes the decision to marry in these early years of the twenty-first century? In terms of raw numbers, the latest figures produced by the Census Bureau reveal that there are some 127.8 million married couples in the United States, or 54.8 percent of the population. If this figure seems surprisingly low, it is because it *is:* the age bracket from which this measurement is gathered includes age-fifteen "adults," and since very few fifteen-year-olds are married, their inclusion in the census surely affects the figure obtained.

However, if you look at the figures for married people who are eighteen-plus years of age, you see an immediate bounce upward in the percentage of married couples; they now constitute 58.1 percent of the population. At ages thirty-five to thirty-nine, a far more significant increase in the number of those living in wedlock appears: married people now number 68.3 percent, almost 70 percent of the population. This upward trend continues over time. At ages fifty to sixty-four, the figure rises to 75.2 percent; and by ages sixty-five to seventy-four, this upward trend reaches its zenith: by now, 76.7 percent of the population is married, according to estimates produced by the 2006 Current Population Study of the U.S. Census Bureau. (The figure given always includes the small number of pairs who are separated but still legally wed.)

So, while the institution of marriage has undergone major assaults and a good deal of flux in the past fifty years, it seems to retain its attraction for an enormous number of people. This is true not only in the United States; it is true worldwide. While rates of wedlock may vary from country to country—and they do—most adults in every known society have married for the past thousand years. In the words of author Kay Hymowitz, "Marriage exists in every known society, no matter how poor or rich; it is what social scientists call a 'human universal.' "

Nevertheless, marriage as the commanding social institution it was in the "togetherness" era of the 1950s—with its formal regulations and strong social norms—has all but disappeared. Becoming a wife or a husband no longer serves to organize and determine the behavior of both members of a wedded pair.

Before the sexual revolution of the 1960s, a time when the women's movement also brought a great many "givens" into question, it was simply assumed that a married woman's role was to run the home and raise the children, while a married man's role was to support the family enterprise financially. A successful marriage was one in which each spouse fulfilled these societal obligations in an acceptable fashion, and it was understood that the spouse/parent's main mission was the rearing of the next generation.

Now, however, finding happiness in the relationship is the marital pair's foremost priority. The modern couple's assessment of their marriage depends on such intangibles as "feelings of satisfaction" and on the sense that their partnership is an emotionally fulfilling one. Marriage, as the clearly defined societal arrangement it once was, no longer exists: being a spouse and being a parent have in some real sense become decoupled from each other. The typical pair's views of what they want from their marriage exist in a far more *personal* realm, and if one or the other member of the couple is intensely disaffected, having had children is no bar to ending the relationship. This is why the institution of marriage currently rests on much shakier ground than it did a half century earlier, in the decade of the 1950s.

It also explains why young adults of the early twenty-first century tend to cast a wary eye upon marriage and often postpone getting married (if they do ever marry) and simply live together instead—an option that would have been unimaginable in their grandparents' generation. Furthermore, if a couple does marry, and the relationship proves ungratifying, there is little social stigma to be weathered in the wake of a marital breakup. Divorce has become a part of normal adult life; it is simply an everyday feature of life in the twenty-first century, especially in America, which has the highest rate of marriage dissolution worldwide.

ALTERNATIVES TO MARRIAGE

The decades following upon the great social ferment of the 1960s saw a steady increase in the rates of cohabitation, out-of-wedlock births and single-parent child-rearing. The meteoric rise of these alternatives to marriage caught a lot of people—including a number of social scientists—by surprise. At the same time, the frequency at which people married showed a decline during the 1970s and 1980s, while the rates of divorce tripled (from 3 percent in 1960 to 9 percent in 1990).

Plainly, the ranks of the married shrank. A recent analysis of the Census Bureau's June 2006 Current Population Study, carried out by sociologist Steven P. Martin, indicated that in the year 1960, 88 percent of men between the ages of thirty-five and forty-four were living in wedlock, while in the year 2005 only 66.2 percent of men in that age-group had tied the marital knot. Similarly, in 1960, 87.4 percent of women between thirty-five and forty-four were married, while in 2005 only 67.2 percent of women between thirty-five and forty-four were living with a wedded mate. The increasing acceptability of divorce and of cohabiting without a marriage license led inevitably to a situation in which, for the first time in human history, many women were raising their children without the presence of an engaged, committed biological mate.

This situation has had a particularly harsh impact on the children of single mothers. As Kay Hymowitz has written, in *Marriage and Caste in America,* children of single parents "are less successful on just about every measure than children living with their married parents regardless of their race, income or education level; they are more prone to drug and alcohol abuse, to crime, and to school failure; they are less likely to graduate from college; they are more likely to have children at a young age, and to do so when they are unmarried." Furthermore, a raft of recent studies documents the fact that youngsters living in families with unrelated adults (for example, a mother and a live-in boyfriend) are at a significantly enhanced risk of suffering physical and/or sexual abuse. One startling 1996 figure, released by the National Incidence Study (a comprehensive federal survey) estimated that children of single parents were at a *77 percent greater risk* of being harmed by physical abuse than were children living with both biological parents. As sociology professor Brad Wilcox of the University of Virginia has observed, "This is the dark underbelly of cohabitation."

Also, scholars of the family have begun taking notice of the glaring economic and social factors at play in terms of which adults do marry and then set about establishing a stable family life. It is now widely recognized that in the wake of the revolutionary era of the 1960s, a phenomenon known as "the marriage gap" has developed. This "gap" refers to the ever-widening chasm between poor, uneducated mothers—who frequently forgo marriage yet go ahead and have children—and their more fortunate sisters, who have the resources and the impetus to postpone childbearing in order to complete their education and develop their careers. The more affluent "haves" on the advantaged side of the marriage gap are eventually able to find suitable husbands and start families. But the less fortunate "have-nots," on the other side of this financial and social chasm, are creating single-parent households without any expectation that an enduring relationship with the biological father will form a part of their own life script.

As the well-known sociologist Andrew Cherlin told me, "Poor people often don't think they have the financial wherewithal to make a marriage work. And if they do marry, their marriages are more frag-ile from the get-go. They never have enough money; they have health problems; they have to deal with the trying, difficult lives of poverty. Obviously, this can cause tensions in a marriage; and it can cause peo-ple to resist marrying in the first place."

At the present time, says family expert Cherlin, the rate of divorce remains relatively stable in the wake of the steep rise that occurred in the closing decades of the last century. Curiously enough, however, it seems to be going *down* among the most educated and *up* among the least educated segments of the population. "The people who are doing better financially—who are, perhaps, the winners in our globalized economy—are getting married more and divorcing less. The people who are doing worse in our economy are marrying less and then divorcing more often." Cultural factors are also intertwined with these monetary factors, for whites and Latinos are predictably more likely to be married than are African-Americans in much the same way as wealthier people are more likely to be married than are the poor.

Does the rate of divorce in the United States persist at the oft-quoted estimate of one in every two marriages? Apparently not. There is no hard-and-fast figure available on what the current divorce rate actually is, but a number of researchers believe that it probably hovers somewhere in the early to mid–40 percent range—which is by no means an insignificant rate of marital breakup. It is also worth noting that half of all divorces occur within the first seven to eight years of a marriage; the Census Bureau quotes year eight as the time of maximum threat. After that watershed, the risk of marital dissolution shows a slow but steady decline; and as time passes the partners are ever likelier to remain together.

INTERVIEWING MARRIED PARTNERS

When I initiated this study, it was with the general goal of sorting out the tasks and challenges that couples over fifty are confronting in these "bonus years" of their lives. I was by no means interested in mounting a controlled statistical study of adults in this age-group; my intent was to be an engaged listener as older couples talked about the salient themes of their lives-in-progress and the issues that were currently on their minds. In the course of this research, I interviewed a large number of over-fifty spouses jointly (roughly speaking, seventy-five). Then, some months later, I returned to talk with a smaller subset of these partners, this time speaking with each member of the pair alone. It may have had something to do with the fact that the couples were in this particular age-group, but I rarely found a gap between what the pair told me when they were together and what each of them told me when the other person wasn't present.

Here is a taste of how these open-ended interviews were conducted: at the outset of the conversation, the first questions I raised were about retirement from an organized work life, and the quest for personally meaningful, purposeful ways to spend time in the aftermath. Discussions of this topic always carry a certain intensity, especially when one member of the pair is retired and the other one is not.

Another set of issues that I would bring up early in a session had to do with the existence of health problems. At these ages, such problems were often minor, but they were *Ping!s*—reminders of time's winged chariot and the fact that the partners were in the third trimester of their lives. Thoughts of mortality, and also silent concerns about the potential illness or loss of the spouse, were, I found, invariably present. These were obviously emotionally loaded subjects for me to raise, but everyone I interviewed acknowledged that they had already given a certain amount of thought to them.

As the discussion continued, I would ask about income and finances. How was money managed, and how were financial decisions made? Did money tend to be a source of tension? Many of my over-fifty volunteers were reasonably comfortable financially, and so concerns about postretirement poverty were not an outstanding issue. Still, there were instances in which money problems were a present and realistic concern.

My next queries were about divorces, deaths and geographical separation from friends and family members. How much satisfaction did the pair derive from their ties with adult children and grandchildren? This could have a profound effect on a couple's sense of success or of failure. Had the partners experienced a "thinning out" in terms of their relationship set and their reliable social resources, as often happens in the later years?

The responses to these latter questions were hugely significant, for aging experts now view social and emotional support to be the sine qua non of well-being and even mortality in the later years. Social isolation is, on the other hand, seen as both psychologically painful and even physically dangerous—a consideration that is stressed more and more often in the current literature on aging.

MARITAL DYNAMICS

As each couple interview evolved, a discussion that was more internal to the state of the marriage began to make its appearance. I typically began this phase by asking the partners to describe the mood-tone of this time of life, and to compare it with earlier periods of their lives together. I asked them if this time segment were a movie or a book, what did they think would be the title? During the course of this work, I received an array of wonderful answers—"Freedom-escence" on more than one occasion; also "Harvest," "Peace" and other titles that were generally in the positive range.

As the conversation continued, I asked about the ways in which the members of the pair had disappointed and surprised each other over the course of time. Then I asked how they had been able to forgive each other's failings and betrayals (if they had been able to do so). Next I asked whether this was a time of increased understanding and renewal or if, on the contrary, there was a sense of having made a peace in place and experiencing increasing emotional distance. These questions were usually responded to with remarkable clarity and frankness.

Lest the reader be wondering, the issue of sex was not left out of the discussion. At some point during the interview I asked: "What do you think are the major sexual issues that emerge at this time of life?" This simple question typically prompted a long and often very involved discussion, one that could move off in unexpected directions.

I should mention that one question most couples seemed to enjoy a great deal was: "What were the smartest moves that each of you ever made? What were the dumbest moves?" I also asked the members of the pair to answer to: "Was I more bad than good? What was good? What was bad?" And I never failed to ask "What role does faith and religion play in your life?" among the other questions covered in the interview.

In regard to inquiries about faith, most respondents described themselves as "deeply spiritual," whether or not they attended a church or temple often or rarely. Finally, I always posed the question: "What were your parents' marriages like at this time of their lives? Do you see any similarities of either set of parents' marriages to your own?" This subject could sometimes pull a total blank, but on other occasions it unearthed a mother lode of rich material. I have often witnessed people's sense of amazement when they recognize the subterranean connections between The Way It Is Now in their present-day lives and The Way It Was in their families of origin.

A TIME OF LIFE

Although I have devoted my entire career to dealing with individuals, couples and families who are in diverse kinds of psychological difficulties, this course of research has carried me in an entirely different direction. What I have encountered in my interviews with couples in their later adulthood is a great deal of what Professor Laura Carstensen calls the "positivity effect": basically, a lot of acceptance and affection being enjoyed by the pair. These people—and I include couples I interviewed twenty years earlier who were *not* doing very well at that time—appear to be at a very good place in their lives.

I don't mean to suggest that the marital partners I've been talking to are not beginning to deal with—or have not already dealt with—a number of demanding concerns. The couples in this book are confronting large questions having to do with retirement, relocation, family connections and, most crucially, what things matter most when the time left to live is shorter than the time that has already gone by. So these mates *do* have big and sometimes confusing issues to negotiate; the important difference that I sense is that they seem to be on the same page as they go about resolving them.

What follows, then, is a series of subjective portrayals of couples age fifty and over; that is, of married partners who are now in this relatively new and unknown stage of living—the additional two-plus to three decades that have made their almost magical appearance in the average span of the human life cycle.

Chapter One

LYNN AND CARL McBRIDE

A GIFT OF TIME

M y interview with the McBrides began—as did all my
interviews—with a short discussion of the "bonus years":
the recent and phenomenal change in the human life
span. I stated that in 1900, in the industrialized West, the average person's life expectancy was not quite fifty years, while in the year 2006
it stood at a record high of 77.6. In a single century, a full thirty years
had been added to the time that the average person could be expected
to live.

In consequence, a new stage has been added to the life cycle—one
that, I suggested, mirrors the adolescent years in terms of the number
of physical, psychological and other life changes that had to be con-
fronted. But unlike adolescence, this later stage of living remained relatively mysterious territory, for its challenges and demands had been
far less researched than had the earlier midlife years and the latter,
declining years (the so-called "old-old" years) near the end of life. The
"bonus years" of fairly healthy later adulthood (the fifties, sixties,

early seventies) were the area that I had marked out for exploration. I
wanted to find out just how people in this age-group were experiencing them.

As I said my little speech, both Lynn and Carl McBride were
nodding their heads as if to say they knew just what I was talking
about. So I took out my digital tape recorder and placed it on the dark
walnut cocktail table between us. Then I opened the large drawing
pad on my lap and turned the pages until I came to one that was
blank.

I was embarking upon the interview, as I always do, by quickly
constructing an outline of the most important facts of the McBrides'
history as a couple. This bare-bones sketch would contain mundane,
ordinary details such as the length of their marriage, the names and
ages of their adult children, the names of their parents and information about which of their parents were still living. I was also filling in
peripheral information about each of their backgrounds, and some
general sense of what their lives in their families of origin had been
like.

In so doing, I was making use of a well-known device called a "family genogram." I have invariably found this clinical tool to be the shortest, safest, most efficient way of gathering an overview of a couple's
emotional and relational biography—a preliminary impression of each
individual's life narrative and major themes, as they'd intertwined
with each other in the making of their unique relationship. For, dry
and factual as these first, commonplace questions posed in the
genogram actually are, they are always laden with rich associations—
associations that begin spilling out in the course of the ensuing discussion. And so the conversation begins.

I FEEL SO RICH!

Lynn McBride, who is a slim, short woman with straight blond Dutch-cut hair, told me that this was a first marriage both for her and her husband, and they had been married for thirty-five years. Carl, who is much taller than his wife, has a rangy physique and a full head of salt-and-pepper hair. He told me he was fifty-nine and Lynn was two years older. The couple had three grown children: two daughters and a son.

All of the McBrides' children were now in their twenties, and all were getting on well in their lives. The older two had graduated from outstanding colleges and were working in New York and Chicago, at jobs they really enjoyed. The youngest was about to graduate from Columbia's Graduate School of Journalism.

The family room we had settled in had a friendly, warm feeling. Carl sat at one end of a long, subtly tweedy sofa scattered with loose back pillows. Lynn sat closer to the other end, with her legs up on the sofa forming a bridge between them. I was seated on one of three large, comfortable chairs that were ranged across the other side. I found myself admiring the lovely worn Isfahan rug that covered the floor beneath this grouping, and which was bordered by an expanse of varnished hardwood floors.

When I asked the couple about their relationships with their now adult children, Lynn was the one to supply the answer. "We get along fine," she said cheerfully. "In fact, just recently they *thanked* me for staying home when they were growing up." I smiled at her, and said that moms rarely receive such outright kudos. She laughed, colored slightly, glanced at her husband in a somewhat ambiguous way, then said, "I agree."

I learned that both the McBrides were accomplished musicians;

Lynn played the flute, but the piano was the major instrument for both of them. At the present time, Carl was a full professor of music at a major Ivy League university in northern New England. Lynn had gone very far in her musical studies—she had both a bachelor's and a master's degree—but had eventually decided that the field didn't suit her.

"I'd always had an interest in psychology and in mental health," she said. "This was true from the time I was a teenager. And as I got older I found myself less and less interested in the music business, so I dropped out before getting my doctorate." She'd wanted to begin her training to be a counselor or social worker immediately, but explained that she couldn't afford to go back to school for a while. "Of course, we lived in North Carolina at the time," she said dryly, as if this were part of a more convoluted explanation.

I let that pass, and asked the couple if they had given any thought to their eventual retirement. Since the typical age of retirement in this country is between sixty and sixty-two, I was surprised to hear that they hadn't. Carl said that he planned to teach until age sixty-five, and maybe seventy. "I will probably teach thirteen to fifteen more years . . . or I plan to." Lynn, who had recently completed a postgraduate fellowship in social work, said she felt closer to the beginning than the end of a career. "I have my first real job in years, and I feel so *rich!*" She was working at an outpatient unit for recently discharged mental patients, most of whom suffered from borderline personality disorder.

Thoughts about retirement were simply not on this couple's horizon. Lynn said she thought that life as a retiree would be altogether boring. "I don't *understand* why people retire!" she declared. But then, after a brief pause, she said musingly, "I suppose there will come a time when I have less energy and want to work part-time. And we're probably going to want to travel, so I'll want more freedom. . . ." Her voice trailed off as if such notions had been reserved for a misty, far-off future. Carl's expression was one of impassive agreement.

The McBrides' responses were unusual, for most couples in their age range tended to answer this question at length, with a stream of stories, fantasies of the future, recollections of the past, accounts of their career experiences. But neither Lynn nor Carl had given any serious consideration to eventually retiring from their careers.

My next questions were about health. Usually, people at their time of life have a complaint of a trivial or, in some instances, a serious sort. In Lynn's case, there had been a real scare—a cancer of the thyroid, one that had been successfully removed several years ago. She was using thyroid replacement hormones and feeling completely like herself. There was no effect on her daily life at all.

"Count your blessings," I said.

"Well, I'm trying," Carl said—a remark I found somewhat perplexing at that moment.

I asked them if they'd ever given thought, as people at our age tend to do (my instinct was that it would be tactful to include myself in this ticklish question), to what life would be like in the absence of the spouse. "I don't think that anybody at these particular ages has any idea how long she or her spouse will live," I added.

There was a pause. "Of course not," Lynn said, while her husband nodded his agreement.

"Do you ever think about that?"

"Yes, I do," Lynn said.

"Yes, for sure," Carl said, almost in unison.

I asked them how they thought that he or she would handle it.

"It's interesting that you should ask that," Lynn said, "because he just got back from a weeklong trip to Toronto, and I was pretty lone-some and I thought about it." She shook her head as if to shake the notion away, then smiled. "The fact is, we expect to live to eighty. But you never know. . . ."

"Anything can happen," Carl said, an apprehensive expression set-tling on his face.

"Yes," I said, "friends start to thin out. . . ." I was thinking of my beloved friend Betsey, who had died recently of pancreatic cancer.

Carl said that hadn't happened to them yet; they hadn't lost close friends of their own generation. "What we've been doing is losing par-ents. Lynn's dad died four years ago, and my dad died a couple of years later." A glance at my sketchbook told me that Lynn's mother had died many years earlier; the McBrides now had just one living parent, Carl's mother.

He told me that she was now living in a retirement village in the midwestern farming community where he grew up; she'd had a life with which she was contented. "She is very secure and happy living in that culture," he said. His tone of voice made it sound as if she were living in a culture that had, over time, grown foreign to him.

I asked Lynn how she thought she would handle things if she were on her own.

"When I think about that, I'm glad I have this career. . . . because I would probably stay real busy, and I suppose I would reach out to friends more. I would probably depend on friends and colleagues far more than I do now," she replied.

I turned to Carl. "How about you?"

He hesitated a long time before responding. "I do think that if Lynn were to go first, I would grieve. . . I would grieve a lot. . . . If she were to go first, it would be very, very difficult. . . ." His voice trailed off.

When I prompted him by asking how he thought he would manage, he simply said, "That's a tough call." He fell silent again, and I
didn't press him further.

At last Lynn said, "We thought of that in regard to our parents—
which one would manage better if the other went first. And it did
come out better, in both cases."

"For both." Carl nodded. "Because her mother died first, and my
dad died first. And in each couple that person was the more problematic member of the couple. By quite a long shot, I think."

"I see," I said, knowing that this was a subject to which we would be
returning.

MONEY

When I asked the McBrides how money was managed, and whether
financial decisions tended to be a source of tension, Carl was the one
to answer. Money had been a *huge* source of tension throughout the
seventeen years they were in North Carolina, he said. "I had a pretty
good academic job, but I was teaching at a state university; and I was
stuck, not making a great salary. And I didn't have that much leverage.
And so Lynn had to work. All through those North Carolina years,
she had her church jobs—playing accompaniment on the piano, leading the choir. And for a while she had a half-time job in the business
school."

I turned to Lynn. "Yet money was a source of tension between the
two of you?"

"Oh, *hugely,*" she assented, repeating the word her husband had
used.

I asked her to give me the outlines of what the money tensions had been about. Lynn shrugged, said that she had always been the one who was looser with money and Carl had always been the tighter one. She thought this had to do with their different backgrounds and their different points of view. "My dad was a Methodist minister, and while he didn't make a lot of money, it was a stable income. Also, he had a master's degree and was respected as a professional in the community. My mother was a college graduate, too, and a professional, as well. And so, while we had to be careful about money, we didn't experience—"

"Your dad handled money extremely well," Carl said.

"My dad handled money pretty well," Lynn agreed. Money had not been a source of anxiety in her family of origin.

I asked Carl to tell me a little more about his own background. "My family was very different from hers. There was much more of a working-class feel to it, and less of a professional feel. Both my parents grew up on farms and went through the difficult times of the Depression. My dad had this medium-size printing business in a small Oklahoma town, and it was our only source of income as my brother and I were growing up. So we didn't have the gentilities that Lynn's family had. Her dad was this Methodist minister, and her mom had grown up in Georgia—she was a sophisticated southern girl who knew the way the world worked. . . . My dad knew what you learn growing up on a farm. . . . His own parents were separated when he was a baby."

"Did you say your grandparents separated when your dad was a baby?" I asked. That addendum seemed to have come out of nowhere.

"Right," Carl said. His father had been fatherless; he'd been raised by his mother alone, and by various aunts and uncles as well. "He got bounced around a lot," Carl said. I had the fleeting thought that his father might have been an illegitimate child.

"Your dad not only got bounced around, but it sounds as if he came from a desperately poor background," I said. "So it's possible that all that anxiety about money was something you inherited from the family's past?" My sentence ended as a question.

"Oh yes," Carl said. Then he frowned and said that the problem often wasn't his father's inability to show a profit in his printing business; it was also his way of making very, very bad decisions about money. "He would hire questionable people and give them a lot of responsibility. The rest of us could see immediately that that was a bad judgment, and eventually, he would lose a lot of money. Or later, he would invest in mutual funds and be taken in by some fast talker."

In short, I thought, unlike Lynn's father, Carl's father had handled money badly.

Is Money a Source of Tension Now?

When it came to handling money and interacting with his wife about the ways she was spending it, Carl's level of anxiety had clearly been very high. It was not the *only* source of tension between them, he said, but it had surely been one of the more dramatic ones—"a real sore spot"—for many, many years.

"Does money continue to be a source of tension now?" I asked them.

Lynn shook her head. "Not so much, no."

"Somewhat?" I was responding to a note of uncertainty in her voice.

"It's not for me," Carl said. And Lynn followed by saying that it was not a source of tension between the two of them. "The reason I might have sounded equivocal," she told me, "is that we're still paying off tuition loans for our kids' education. Because we couldn't afford it as they went through."

"Well, we've paid some off, but we borrowed a lot," Carl said. "And we're dealing with that debt right now. But I don't think we have much tension about money, for a number of reasons. Both of us have grown a lot, emotionally. And it doesn't hurt to be teaching at a first-rate university and making a pretty good salary," he added, with a smile.

"And fortunately, what I'm making at my new job is going to help pay off the tuition," Lynn said. "So that's a good feeling for me."

I looked from one to the other. "Then I gather that you're both on the same page about handling money, at this point. Money is not a source of quarrels—is that right?"

Lynn and Carl turned to each other, exchanged a questioning glance, then turned back and nodded confidently to me.

A TIME OF DESPAIR

There are some questions that I usually reserve for the latter part of the interview. Questions such as *How have you been able to forgive each other's failings and betrayals (if there have been any)?* can on occasion elicit a flood of highly sensitive, emotional material. I had expected nothing of the sort to happen when I asked the McBrides about their relations with their adult children. Their earlier reports about their children had sounded as if things were going well.

But Carl said, "The critical thing—the question about the kids brings it up—" He stopped.

I shook my head as if to say I didn't understand. Then he explained that in the months preceding their move from North Carolina he had been unable to decide whether he wanted to remain where he was or take the new, more prestigious and better-paying job in the North. "I went back and forth, back and forth, in making that decision, and it was a terribly tense time for all of us. Lynn and I were fighting a lot; she and the kids wanted to go . . . and eventually we did leave North Carolina. But as soon as we arrived, I had a huge reaction, and I got severely depressed."

There was a silence, which I ended by asking quietly, "A kind of buyer's remorse?"

He nodded. "A buyer's remorse for this house, which was in terrible shape when we moved in." Carl paused, looked contentedly around the sunny, pretty living room, with its white-painted walls and carved ceiling moldings. "But remorse mostly for the job. I spent three years dying to go back—so much so that I got three offers in a row to go back to essentially the same job."

It was clear that he'd been desperately homesick. But Lynn and the children were staunchly opposed to going back.

"So somehow I was able to hold on and stay here," Carl continued. "Which in retrospect was the better thing to do. It was right. We're all in much better shape than we would have been if I'd either stayed in North Carolina in the first place or especially if we had gone back. There was no *way* of going backward . . . we couldn't . . ."

Something in his tone made me ask: "So you people were on the edge of separating . . . or divorcing . . . ?"

"Yes," Lynn said, shortly.

"Yes," Carl echoed.

"And this went on over a three-year period?" I asked.

Carl shook his head, said that it had actually been a five-year period, during which his depression became so severe that he spent a month in the university's inpatient psychiatric unit. This suggested to me that he must have been actively suicidal for a period of time.

When I asked him if that had been the case, he nodded. "Before the hospital time I *was*—that's why I went in."

I put my pencil down on my sketchbook, looked from Carl to Lynn and then back to Carl. He had a calm expression on his face, and looked well-muscled—as if he were physically fit and in no way drained of vigor. "You seem to be in great shape now," I said. "It's amazing to hear of this."

"I *am* in great shape," Carl said. "But back then, the torment—my own personal torment—was unbearable. Somehow I managed to do my job—to teach well—but it was a struggle to even gather the energy and momentum to even drive back and forth to my classes. Later, after I got out of the hospital, I didn't feel suicidal anymore. But I was so worn down, so depleted."

Had any of the medications that are now available been of any help to him? I asked.

"He is very resistant to medications," Lynn said evenly.

Carl nodded, but said he suspected that his current antidepressant—one of the older ones called nortriptyline—might be helping him somewhat. He wasn't sure. "Still, the upshot of all this was that one day, about three years ago come November, I woke up and—just like that—I felt like myself. And I haven't felt depressed since that time." He smiled at me, looking almost jubilant, an expression that brought a look of pleasure to his wife's face.

I smiled back, reminded him that this whole discussion had arisen when I'd asked them about the children. "So tell me about the kids," I prompted.

"Okay, you're right," Carl said. "And the reason that your question about the kids brought this up was that through all of this, they have been absolutely wonderful. I think we have basically no complaints.

We feel very fortunate that they are as happy as they are, and that they're doing so well, and things are working out so well for them. . . . Because obviously, as they were growing up, there were a lot of tensions in the family around various things."

Money had been one of them, that was clear to me. Where the family lived had also been an issue. I wondered what the other concerns had been, and what had cast this husband, father and respected professional into so profound and prolonged a depressive state.

HER ANGER

When I asked the McBrides how each of them had disappointed and surprised the other, over time, Lynn reared back in her seat. It was almost as if I'd been playing catch with Carl and had suddenly thrown the ball in her direction.

"I know," I said sympathetically, "that question's a dog, isn't it?"

"Boy, that *is* a loaded question," she said. "Whew! Well, do you want to go first?" she asked her husband. Then she said, "You go first."

Carl paused momentarily, as if to gather his thoughts. "Over time, the way in which Lynn disappointed me—going way back, and early in the marriage—was that she just seemed to have a lot of anger. So that I would feel that our relationship was going along quite well, and then something would happen—it was like some sort of spark—and she would jump all over me. And this went on for years and years, and it was really always iffy. Not that we didn't have a lot of good times—we did—but there were a lot of things that weren't working."

"So you felt you had to tiptoe around her?" I asked.

He nodded. "Right. And the thing was . . ." He hesitated before continuing. "I think that our relationship was really affected by things we brought to the marriage from our families of origin. And I don't want to dwell on it, but I think there's something that affected our marriage in a very significant way, and was at the root of the depression . . . which was that I was sexually abused for six years while I was growing up."

Taken aback, I murmured, "By whom?" My own thought was that six years, in the life of a growing child, is a very long time. And was it his anger, or his wife's anger, that we'd been discussing?

Carl said shortly, "It was a neighbor," and his tone of voice suggested that we'd better leave it there. I sat still, saying nothing.

After a few moments, Carl went on to say that he had held this secret to himself all the way through high school and beyond. "I'd told Lynn about it, and I thought that I had dealt with it, but I hadn't. And that's what ultimately made me so vulnerable when we moved here. And so early on, especially in the North Carolina years, one of the ways Lynn disappointed me was that I thought everything in my life was wonderful—that we had great kids and a terrific family and that she and I had a wonderful relationship—but it was clear that Lynn didn't believe that. She kept seeing real problems and feeling a lot of dissatisfaction with me."

Carl went on to say that he had re-created a situation that existed in his high school days: one in which he was seen as a kind of golden boy—talented, smart, much admired. "I hadn't realized that that situation was actually very destructive. To *me*."

I asked him in what ways the situation had been destructive, and he turned to Lynn and asked her to answer. "It was destructive for me in the sense that Carl was really married to his career and an image of himself that he had in his head. . . . I mean, officially we did have a good life, and a lot of it was solid, but a lot of it was not very real."

"You mean it was a fictional good life?" Both of them laughed and nodded.

Then I said, "But if I could stop you for a moment, I'm puzzled by the fact that you, Lynn, are the angry one and you, Carl"—I turned to him—"had a lot to be angry about, as an abused child . . . ?"

"Oh yeah," Lynn said, in a wry tone of voice. "It's called Projective Identification." And she gave me a knowing smile, which I returned.

In my first book on marriage—a book about couples ranging in age from late adolescence to their late forties—I had popularized the concept of Projective Identification. Despite its alarmingly complicated-sounding name, this concept refers to a rather simple and quite prevalent psychological device in which one member of a pair pawns off on the other member whatever traits or feelings he or she can't admit to—in Carl's case, anger. He saw Lynn as all too prone to anger, while he was conscious of no anger within himself.

To put it differently, Lynn "carried the anger" for both of them, while Carl saw himself as completely devoid of angry feelings. Lynn was the "voice of anger" in their troubled relationship, and Carl felt critical of her even as he identified with her expression of his own disavowed, deeply buried rage.

Carl nodded, said, "Right."

"Is that what was going on?" I asked the pair of them.

"Yes," Lynn said. "Oh yes. Because Carl's family do not do anger at all."

A SECOND-CLASS CITIZEN

I turned to Carl, who nodded in agreement. He said that he was now able to feel his anger—and assert himself, if necessary—but that getting to this point had been a long, hard process. "I could never have owned up to this a number of years ago, but having this whole 'perfect family' thing blasted to bits when we moved north was ultimately good in the long run. Because it revealed all the bad stuff that I was contributing to the marriage, and it ultimately uncovered all this bad stuff that was inside *me*. . . . And this gave us the opportunity to work it through."

Lynn was leaning forward in her seat, as though impatient for a chance to speak. "And I guess your disappointment was his marriage to his career? Is that right?" I asked her.

"Yes, the marriage to the career and the fact that I never felt that I was at the top of Carl's priority list. I felt like I was down a ways. . . . And then, when the kids came along, I felt that I was even under *them*." There was indignation in her voice at this moment.

Carl said that when they first moved into their new home in New England, they'd started having horrible fights, and Lynn kept saying that she felt like a second-class citizen. "I think that somehow moving up here made her realize that for many years, while we were in North Carolina, she'd felt like a second-class citizen and been *treated* like one. But when we were living there, she hadn't been able to articulate it—"

"Because the culture, when we were in the South, supported the myth," Lynn interrupted him. "Carl had people all over that community eating out of his hand, and that culture did not allow me to have equal status with him. And so by definition I was a few steps down, so anytime I tried to assert myself I just got smashed. Because I was being non-feminine or too ballsy or whatever." She smiled and shrugged.

Then she explained that while she and her husband were both classical pianists, she was a much stronger performer and he was a much stronger intellectual. But when they lived in North Carolina, neither of them was ever asked to do major performances in the university's concert hall. Regardless of this fact, Carl enjoyed widespread respect and had the reputation of being a fabulous performer. "I didn't get recognized at all for what I could do in music. It was subtle but it was a really macho atmosphere, so people in our social circle simply couldn't accept the fact that I was *good*."

SURPRISES

I asked the McBrides about the ways they had surprised each other, over time.

"Maybe this is a terrible thing to say," responded Lynn, "but *my* biggest surprise has been the way that Carl has turned himself around. Since the depression. Not just in terms of his mood, but the way he is in our relationship. Because, frankly, to be perfectly honest"—she paused and addressed Carl directly—"I don't think this is any news to you"—then turned back to me—"by the time the kids were teenagers, I thought this was going to be over. I was prepared for that, because I thought, 'Nothing is ever going to change.' And I was not content to live in a one-, two- or three-down position for the rest of my life.

"So when we came here and Carl got depressed and wanted to go right back to North Carolina, knowing that I had been aching to get out of there for the past fourteen or fifteen years . . ."

"That's kind of a low estimate." Carl laughed.

"So when the first thing he says to me, almost literally, is that he wants to go back there, I could not believe my ears. So I thought, 'This is over. This is just *over.*' "

Lynn's big surprise, she reiterated, was her husband's capacity to surmount what had happened to him, and where he had come from. But he *has*, she said, with a smile.

What had surprised Carl was far less sweeping, and it had happened slowly as he began to feel better and the relationship was improving. "I would say some trivial thing that in the past Lynn would have jumped at me for, and she wouldn't jump at me. And that's happened any number of times, and it's been a pleasant surprise.

"I didn't really register this early on, but I've felt for many years that she was incredibly dissatisfied. That somehow things weren't working right for her . . . that she was capable of a far more intimate relationship than I was. Part of it was her own personality, part of it was that I was just so frightened and terrified after the six years of abuse that I just couldn't *give*, emotionally. In that way, the depression was a good thing, because I have learned how to do that. I mean, I don't want to speak for her, but I *do* think we have an excellent relationship now."

I turned, met Lynn's gaze. "Well, would you agree?"

"Yes," she answered, without hesitation.

THIS TIME OF LIFE

I asked the McBrides what name they would give this particular phase of their lives.

When neither of them responded, I prompted them by saying, "Adolescence has a certain mood-tone associated with it. A time of some turmoil, and of changes—in bodies, in outlook, in a variety of external circumstances—and this time of life is similar in certain ways. So if you think of it in terms of a movie or a book, what would you call it?"

Lynn said, "*The New Beginning.*" I nodded, thinking that for her, at age sixty-one, this was true in many ways.

Carl said, "*Peace,* I think."

"So for both of you, it's in the positive range?" I asked him.

"Yes, very *strongly* so." He smiled, and his wife nodded her agreement.

The Bonus Years

As I sat there, I reflected that before the remarkable shift in health and longevity that this past century has witnessed, a couple such as the McBrides were likely to have been in their elderly/ill/dying years. After all, Carl was now in his late fifties and Lynn in her early sixties; but here they were before me, looking healthy and content. It was clear that Carl had benefited greatly from the extended therapy he'd received in the course of his depression, for he had exorcised the demons of childhood sexual abuse that had haunted him throughout his life. Although early on he'd believed that he had "dealt with those events" by repressing them, they had prevented him from being a real, authentic human being, capable of being truly intimate with his wife.

And Lynn had sensed this but had been unable to reach him. She'd had "my own problems with mild depression," she admitted in the course of the interview. These problems had been due to a chilly, disapproving mother and an emotionally distant, frustrating husband; in short, to an inability to make real human contact with those who should have been closest to her.

At the outset of the twentieth century, it occurred to me, this pair would have been unlikely to outlive their mutual dissatisfaction—not only with the course their individual lives had taken but with the lives they had lived together. So, despite the pain the McBrides had endured as they underwent so many major life upheavals—his job change, their move north, his depression—these extra decades of health and well-being had become a "bonus," in every possible sense of that word. For it was *time* that had allowed for this profound transformation in the couple's relationship.

Chapter Two

DOES DIVORCE MAKE
PEOPLE HAPPY?

ynn McBride had said that the biggest way in which her husband had surprised her, over the course of their marriage, was
the manner in which he'd turned himself, and the tenor of their
relationship, completely around. Before that time, her resentful, angry
thoughts had been focused on *getting out*. Now she wasn't simply
responding to the amelioration of her spouse's self-absorbed, endlessly
depressed mood but to the newly tender way he was in their relationship. He was emotionally available to her, capable of being intimate.
Before these changes happened, Lynn had reached the decision that by
the time the kids were teenagers, the marriage was going to be *over*.
She was convinced that nothing was ever going to change; she'd stated
firmly, "And I was not content to live in a one-, two- or three-down
position for the rest of my life."

This raises a fundamental question: *Would divorce have made Lynn
McBride happy—either earlier in the marriage, or later on, after the children had left?* The widely held assumption is that a person who leaves
an unhappy marriage will be better off than the one who grits her

teeth and decides to stick it out. But a remarkable study, first reported in June 2002, actually looked at this assumption empirically, and the results they came up with were nothing shy of startling.

This research project, whose lead investigator was University of Chicago professor of sociology Linda J. Waite, was mounted with the purpose of studying a phenomenon that nobody had ever actually examined observationally before: the *aftermath* of divorce—on the divorcing mates themselves, not on their children. Given that people who were separated or getting divorced considered the marriage their major problem, the question was: Were these individuals happier five years later, considering that the problem (the miserable marriage) was now some period of time behind them?

Researcher Waite and her collaborators made use of a large nationally representative survey (the National Survey of Families and Households) and identified a subgroup of the 5,232 married adult respondents who'd rated their marriages as unhappy. That is, on a 7-point scale ranging from 1, *very unhappy* (the lowest), all the way up to 7, *very happy* (the highest), these spouses gave their marriages a dismally low 1 or 2 rating (*very unhappy* or *not too happy*). There was a total of 645 dissatisfied mates in this survey, which was carried out in the late 1980s.

The National Survey of Families and Households typically follows the representative sample over the subsequent five-year period. Within that space of time, the lives of the identified subset of 645 unhappy partners unfolded in a variety of ways. Some divorced; some became separated; some got divorced and remarried; some were widowed; and some simply remained married to the original mate. So the question was: *Which of these people—all of whom had been unhappily married on the initial survey—were doing better five years later?*

Naturally one might assume that those who had divorced in the interim would be better off, having experienced the relief of putting their distressing marriages behind them. Given that the marriages' ending had been seen as the only possible solution to their problems, the transition to divorce would presumably have positive effects in terms of their emotional well-being. But when the researchers looked at those unhappy spouses who had divorced in the interim, they found that, by and large, these people had *not* reaped the expected psychological benefits.

On the contrary, on a variety of measures about which they had been queried originally—such as depressive symptoms, anxiety, levels of self-esteem, sense of personal mastery, etc.—the divorcées and divorcés didn't look much better than they had looked earlier, during their marriages. In fact, some of them looked worse. The striking—indeed, counterintuitive—conclusion that these social scientists arrived at was that unhappily married adults who divorced or separated were *no happier*, on average, than unhappily married adults who stayed married to the same partner.

Of course, the conventional wisdom—something that, generally speaking, many of us subscribe to—is that getting a divorce is better than staying in an unhappy marriage. It is well known that people in bad marriages get into more domestic disputes with their spouses and often suffer from psychological difficulties of all kinds, such as depression, anxiety disorders, phobias and the like. Getting out of this sorry situation would seem to make the best of sense.

Nevertheless, after analyzing the five-year data on a number of psychological measures—including overall happiness, self-esteem, hostility, autonomy, a sense of purpose in life, self-acceptance and drinking behaviors—the Waite researchers found that on these compelling measures, the divorce had made no difference at all. Divorcing, on average, failed to improve the emotional well-being of unhappily married people.

As the team reported, "only one out of five unhappy spouses who divorced or separated had happily remarried in the same time period." This meant that, statistically speaking, a mere 20 percent of those individuals who had divorced or separated within this five-year time frame had "lived happily ever after"—that is, improved their lives and their emotional well-being within the five-year time frame.

On the other hand, many of those who stayed in their marriages had fared surprisingly well. To their own astonishment, the Waite group found that two out of three of the *unhappily* married adults who'd avoided separation ended up *happily married* five years afterward. In their thoughtful analysis, the researchers wrote:

> If only the worst marriages end in divorce, one would expect greater psychological benefits from divorce. Instead, looking at changes in emotional and psychological well-being, we found that unhappily married adults who divorced were no more likely to report emotional and psychological improvement than those who stayed married. In addition, the most unhappy marriages reported the most dramatic turnarounds. Among those who rated their marriages as very unhappy, almost eight out of 10 who avoided divorce were happily married five years later.

Did such "marital turnarounds" have to do with the fact that some outside stressors, which might have been transitory, had been resolved during the intervening space of time?

I thought of the McBrides' situation, in which a seemingly *favorable* turn of events—Carl's sudden rise in academic status to an Ivy League professorship, along with a considerable increase in salary—had triggered a depression that lasted, on and off, for a number of years. Apparently this new position was one to which Carl had felt himself intellectually (and in some deep sense, morally) unequal. Lynn might have felt justified in leaving the marriage at that point, telling herself that the relationship had not been truly satisfactory for a very long time, and that in recent years it had become intolerable. But she hadn't done so . . . and when that highly stressful period ended, the marriage turned itself around.

The Focus Groups (1)

After their formal analysis of the varying pathways through life taken by the 645 couples in the 1988 NSFH survey, Waite et al. decided to look in greater depth at those self-described unhappy partners whose marriages had not only endured but had even improved during that five-year interval.

The questions they explored were various and intriguing: for instance, what had made the couples' relationships unhappy in the first place? How had these troubled mates avoided separation or divorce? Who or what did they believe helped turn their marriages around, so that they were happier five years later?

In order to collect more information on these resilient pairs—however anecdotal and tentative in nature—the scholars set up four focus groups, consisting of fifty-five couples in toto. The marital narratives they heard in the various groups, Waite et al. reported, "surprised and intrigued us." As they slowly compiled the stories of how the marriages became unhappy originally, the problems appeared to fall into three broad categories: (1) when bad things happen to good spouses; (2) men behaving badly; and (3) communication difficulties and difficult personality traits. These classifications do cover the marital-misery waterfront.

As one example of the first kind of marital difficulty, termed "when bad things happen to good spouses," the authors cited a couple whose son had gone through a long period of involvement in drugs. This situation disturbed the parents so severely that it became a problem between them. "Just the frustration on both our parts about how to deal with it," the husband reflected. "Just the incredible tension brought on us." This outside stressor had taken a ten-year chunk out of the couple's twenty-six-year marriage.

The second category ("men behaving badly") contained narratives of infidelity (real or emotional); being overly critical; belittling or controlling their spouses; alcoholism; spending too much time away from the family or simply "checking out." Interestingly enough, in this particular sample, very few wives and no husbands saw the wife's behavior as chiefly to blame. One of the many examples of this male "bad behavior" was that reported by a military husband, who shamefacedly described his years of alcohol abuse and acting out as follows: "Macho drinking, cussing, fighting at the drop of a hat . . . I wasn't physically abusive, but I was verbally abusive without knowing it."

The third category ("communication difficulties and difficult personality traits") consisted of those relationships marked by chronic conflict, emotional neglect and problems in talking and listening to the partner empathically and accurately. One husband reported that after the children came his wife "got old real fast. I'm a happy-go-lucky guy. I want to go out and have a good time. When I met her, she was wild. She got too responsible, too regimented. She's like my grandmother."

Couples in this category were dealing not only with communication issues and problematic personality traits but with differences in lifestyle philosophies. With some exceptions, partners in this group were less likely to report dramatic turnarounds in marital happiness. They'd simply learned to live more amicably with the background hum of ongoing complaints about—or from—the spouse.

Or, in some instances, they developed a newfound sense of freedom and autonomy. As one wife told the interviewer, her overbearing, critical husband was silenced when she threatened divorce, started speaking up for herself and developed interests and friendships outside the marriage.

"I answered him back. I got 'the Mouth.' I was the one who did the changing. If I wanted to go out with the girls, I went out. I got *wings*."

The Nature of Commitment

Given the seriousness of some of the marital woes described—such as infidelity, alcoholism, etc.—that many of these unhappy couples had experienced, the focus group participants were asked why they hadn't separated or divorced. As Waite et al. reported:

> The answers ranged from children's need for fathers, to money, marriage vows, religious and family norms, friendship, and the couple's personal love story. . . . We were struck, however, by the generally low opinion many of these survivors of unhappy marriages had of divorce. . . . [W]hen divorce thoughts arose, they tended to compare the trials and tribulations of marriage to what they saw as the even greater trials and tribulations of divorce.

Along with the couples' professed reasons for remaining together, though, the scholars recognized that another, more ephemeral factor was at play in all these marital situations. It is the much-researched yet somewhat elusive factor that distinguishes the large number (recent estimates are in the 43 to 47 percent range) of American couples who divorce from the large number who elect to stay together—and this factor is called *commitment*.

What does it mean to be committed to a relationship? What is understood about the basic nature of commitment?

PERSONAL COMMITMENT

In a 1999 paper published in the *Journal of Marriage and the Family*, sociologists Michael Johnson et al. pointed out that most people understand the word "commitment" in the sense of "personal commitment." By this is meant: really *wanting* to stay in a relationship; feeling happy with the partner; in love with (or at least liking) him or her; experiencing one's identity as being wrapped up in continuance of the marriage—in brief, feeling a sense of personal dedication to the mate.

Clearly, this is a very positive motivation, one that springs from an individual's inner feelings about his or her partner, and the intimate bond that they have forged together and they share.

MORAL COMMITMENT

However, as these social scientists point out, an individual's commitment to a relationship can spring from other, very different sources. For example, a second and different motive for remaining committed to a marriage can be a sense of *moral obligation*. This kind of commitment, like "personal commitment," springs from feelings that are internal to the self. But in this case, they are "ought" and "should" kinds of feelings. A sense of constraint pervades the relationship, the sense that it is one's duty to stay in the relationship whether one really likes the relationship or not.

Moral commitment exerts its strongest power when the individual is dissatisfied and no longer has a personal commitment to a relationship. He or she may be considering leaving but feel restrained on ethical grounds. In such situations the person's thinking may be: "I really shouldn't consider doing this; it would be morally wrong to abandon this partner whom I've taken on as a lifetime obligation. I'm not happy with the relationship, but I feel committed to sticking with it."

Another, very powerful force at play might be the individual's sense of moral obligation to the people who would be hurt if he or she left the relationship. Children are always a major consideration; often, one hears of unhappy spouses who stay in a marriage for the sake of their offspring. An example of this was heard in one of the focus group settings, where one woman explained why she had decided not to divorce: "Because of my child. I could have taken her back with my family in Germany, but I think a child is better off with a mom and a dad."

Most important in this kind of situation is the individual's moral obligation to the partner and the offspring. A person may be unhappy with the relationship yet feel that even though he doesn't love his partner anymore, it would hurt her and/or his children too cruelly if he were to leave. So he stays in the relationship for that conscientious, ethical reason.

As Johnson et al. point out, an integral part of this decision is often based on a person's need to maintain a sense of internal consistency— a sense of who he or she really *is*. If an individual feels that leaving the partner is a despicably wrong thing to do, then jettisoning the relationship would affect his sense of worth and self-respect. For this kind of reason, he might say to himself, "I'm not the kind of person who repudiates important vows or promises I've undertaken; and since I've taken this on as a lifetime relationship, I'm going to stick to it and make it work out."

Clearly, in a morally obligated commitment, the pressure to remain would *not* be coming from real preference, but from the sense that one could not live comfortably with oneself if one behaved in ways that were inconsistent with one's own beliefs and values—and these would include sparing close others from emotional suffering and distress.

STRUCTURAL COMMITMENT

Still a third type of motive for remaining in a relationship involves what Johnson et al. term a "structural commitment." Unlike a personal or moral commitment, a structural commitment has to do with external forces that act to constrain (or "trap") a spouse in the relationship, whether he or she wants to stay there or not. A structural type of commitment is based on the feeling that there are things *outside* the person that would make it very difficult for him or her to leave the partner.

In this type of situation, remaining in the relationship has very little to do with an individual's real, inner attachment to the spouse, in terms of either a personal or a moral obligation. This type of commitment involves an assessment of the *costs* of leaving the relationship—and one set of costs would have to do with what Johnson et al. call "termination procedures," i.e., the very process of getting out.

A person might think, "What would I have to do to leave this relationship?" His or her deliberations might then revolve around going through all the legal procedures surrounding a divorce, and the very real possibility that treasured assets—the family home and its contents, for example—might have to be sold. These concerns might well feel like major hurdles that he or she simply doesn't want to deal with. Furthermore, if the individual contemplating a divorce is a nonworking wife with few marketable skills, she might have realistic worries about how she will be able to support herself and also care for her children, if she has them. On the other hand, if the person is a husband, he might contemplate a future in which he wouldn't have easy access to his children and in which his meaningful relationships with them could be starkly affected, even ruined.

Moreover, if the contemplated divorce would inevitably involve selling the family home, the kids might be terribly upset by having to leave their old, well-known neighborhood and move to different, unfamiliar schools. Thus, the person who feels neither personally nor morally obligated to remain in the relationship might nevertheless have to consider the many ways in which life would change if he or she did so.

Another, very important aspect of a structural commitment has to do with alternatives to the current union. A worry that often preoccupies people most when they think about leaving their spouse is "Will I ever have another relationship? Am I marriageable? Can I find another mate who will even be as good as the (unsatisfactory) one I have?" Unless there is a dedicated replacement partner already waiting in the wings, these considerations are typically the cause of considerable, often reality-based trepidation.

Still another factor often present in this type of commitment has to do with plain old social or religious pressure. When people start talking to friends or relatives about the possibility of divorce—or even when they *imagine* what other people would say if they *did* talk about it!—they feel apprehensive about the disapproving, or even condemning, reactions of others. As sociologists Johnson et al. write: "Friends and relatives may, for either moral or pragmatic reasons, put pressure on an individual to stick with a relationship that seems headed for dissolution. When such pressures come from people whose opinions matter, individuals may feel constrained to continue a relationship even when they feel little personal or moral commitment."

Of course, there is a wide array of lifestyle and community variables when it comes to individuals and the social structure in which they are embedded. If a person is surrounded by devout Catholics who don't believe in divorce, she or he is going to experience more censure and criticism than someone who happens to be situated in a less traditional religious milieu. In the latter case, there obviously won't be as much horrified, disapproving social pressure.

But the forces that constrain a person to remain in a marriage surely don't have to spring from religious sources alone. I can recall interviewing a forty-seven-year-old woman—a genuine Boston Brahmin—for my book *Secrets, Lies, Betrayals*. This woman told me her deepest secret, which was that she loathed her husband in every way, totally and completely. She made this confidence with so much barely controlled rage that I asked her if she had ever given thought to leaving him. She didn't hesitate: that would be impossible, she said. When I asked her why, she explained that in the social milieu in which she moved, divorcing her husband would mean that she would never be invited to a dinner party again. In the elite, conservative world in which she lived, leaving her spouse would mean that her whole life as she knew it would be over. The fundamental truth—which she anticipated in a realistic way—was that she would be abandoned by those around her.

Finally, an important and similarly constraining "structural" factor can have to do with the sobering thought of all the time and energy that has already been poured into the relationship. Will all the shared history that has gone before—the good things along with the bad—be seen as thoroughly *wasted* if the relationship dissolves, and the happy parts of their shared past are poured down memory's drain? Even though a dissatisfied spouse may be neither personally nor morally committed to the partner, the idea of negating the pair's years together may be perceived as a painful waste—an act that would involve, for one or both partners, the sense of losing an irretrievable investment. Curiously enough, this consideration often carries an unexpected amount of weight when it comes to deciding whether or not to remain in the relationship.

THE MARITAL TURNAROUNDS

As they sifted through the vivid, gripping stories told by the couples in their focus groups, the Waite researchers recognized that many of the difficulties these partners had experienced five years earlier were initiated by outside stressors (e.g., "structural" problems) that had affected the relationship in negative, destructive ways. "Many spouses we interviewed who survived marital unhappiness did not see problems with the relationship as the cause," the researchers wrote. "Instead they blamed outside forces for causing both unhappiness and relationship stress: Spouses became ill, lost jobs [and] got depressed, children got into trouble or created marital stresses by their financial and emotional demands."

One husband reported a low point when a client of his went bankrupt and he himself lost $40,000 in commissions. Several men talked about the birth of a first or second child as a hard time, triggering conflict with their wives, who resented the time they spent away from the family, the added financial stresses or both. One spouse actually blamed the weather in Florida! He said, "It was turning me into a madman. She couldn't deal with it. I was very agitated, no tolerance for anything. The heat just really got to me."

Wives also blamed outside stressors, although this was a less prominent theme in their narratives. One woman talked about a period when her husband, an independent contractor, suffered a hand injury and was unemployed for a year. He stopped talking, she said, "and I'm a big talker." She would ask him what was wrong, and he would say that nothing was wrong. "You're doing nothing but staring at a wall, what do you mean nothing's wrong? The kids are avoiding you, you look like you are in a coma."

He said, "Can't I be miserable?" and she said, "Yeah, but for how long?"

Both husbands and wives emphasized the hardships of married life, the stress coming from their work worlds, the time and resources taken up by children. It would have been much easier, observed the Waite scholars, to have imagined that the unhappy spouses in their original sample would end up divorced rather than as 6, *happy,* or 7, *very happy,* on the national survey five years later!

But comments from one set of husbands (an affluent, more educated focus group hailing from a northern Virginia suburb) sounded like this: "We've reached the 'like and comfort' stage. You understand one another." Another man said, "You can almost read each other's mind. If I weren't married, I'd have more money, but aside from that I'd be lonesome. Guys have this fantasy of being free to go out to the Super Bowl together. But after you do, you have nothing to come home to."

In the scholars' mainly blue-collar New Jersey focus group, talk about the joys of partnership often appeared. "Building a life together. Everything we did, we did together," said one husband, who'd been married for forty years. "We really enjoy each other," said another, "and our kids give us a lot of joy." And still another husband said, "You rely on each other. Like when you have the flu or are sick. It's miserable getting along by yourself."

As for the wives, they "described relationships that ranged from the merely functional to warm family partnerships up through still-passionate love affairs," wrote the Waite researchers.

Some of the *worst* marriages appeared to undergo the most remarkable turnarounds. For example, men who had behaved badly and later regretted it were deeply grateful to their forgiving spouses. One husband, whose relationship had survived a tumultuous period of serious drinking, hanging out in bars and sexual cheating, said that his marriage had "probably saved my life." As he related, "When I was younger, I was a pretty wild sort of a guy. Drinking, driving, going across the country. Sometimes I look back and think, 'God must have had a plan for me, so many places where I might have died.' Marriage kind of settled me down. I got roots with my wife and family."

WHAT HELPED?

How and why had these formerly unhappy marriages improved? The most commonplace answer to this question that the scholars received was simply: "Time passed." Problems that had once seemed insurmountable—job situations, troubled children, chronic difficulties of all sorts—either eased up or were simply seen with a fresh perspective. As one spouse put it, "We talked. But mostly we put one foot in front of the other." The Waite group called this approach "the marital endurance ethic."

Another strategy was what Waite et al. termed the "marital work ethic." This might involve getting helpful outsiders into the act— either trained therapists, as the McBrides did, or pastoral counselors and/or close family relatives. One husband, who credits clergy assistance with ending his chronic infidelity to his wife, said he was now a changed person. "I open up a little more, let my wife know what's bothering me; and I provide more of a sympathetic ear to her own problems also." In instances where the marital work ethic prevails, putting serious effort and energy into the relationship serves as the key to its improvement.

Still a third way of turning the situation around was what the researchers termed the "personal happiness ethic." In such instances, the spouses had ceased struggling to change each other or to strengthen the relationship; rather, they'd managed to improve their own separate, individual lives. Without either ending or renovating their problematic marriages, the mates had simply settled for an amicable coexistence and gone about pursuing their own friendships and interests without getting in their partners' way. Examples of the personal happiness ethic would be a husband who said, "Travel helps keep me interested. If I were in the house constantly, I have to be honest, I'd be gone." Another would be the woman quoted previously who said she got "the Mouth," acquired her own friendships and pursuits, and declared proudly that she "got wings."

THE ESCAPE HYPOTHESIS

Because the Waite report, circulated in 2002, appeared to carry such a conspicuous anti-divorce message, many social scientists' eyebrows were raised. It was published by the Institute for American Values, an organization well known in the scholarly community for being dedicated to the preservation of the institution of marriage. Were the Waite report's numbers "cooked" or computed in such a way that divorce looked like a chancy, precarious idea—aside from the sole exception the researchers cited, which was when domestic violence was part of the marital scene?

A great deal of debate and dissension swirled around the Waite report's publication, but its major conclusions were never overturned. Meanwhile, an arresting new postulate about marriage and divorce was being investigated by several groups of researchers. This was the so-called escape hypothesis—the theory that there is an interaction between the quality of a marriage and an ex-spouse's sense of well-being after the marriage has ended. The basic assumption being made is that the more awful the marriage has been, the more relief the divorced person will experience in its aftermath. And, therefore, the fewer adverse effects (e.g., symptoms of depression or anxiety) will be experienced after the marital breakup.

Earlier on, I listed the many fears and worries about termination procedures that can keep an unhappy spouse locked into a structural commitment. But when a person has actually left the marriage and begun divorce proceedings, she or he often meets a great deal of distress and turbulence that were not actually anticipated. For instance, there may be unforeseen custody disputes; the pain of losing friends who side with your ex-partner; financial problems that mount up almost exponentially; the burden of taking over the household tasks that the spouse used to perform; a sense of loneliness that has to do with the loss of the spouse's company, however unpleasant; and so forth.

But according to the escape hypothesis, *the huge sense of relief* a person experiences after leaving a deeply troubled, conflicted relationship will serve to counter—or perhaps cancel out—many of the disadvantages and liabilities that a divorce is known to entail. This theory seems to make good sense and has a naturally intuitive appeal.

However, several studies of the relationship between the quality of a certain marriage and the effects of its dissolution on an ex-spouse's well-being produced varying, inconclusive results. Moreover, the number of subjects involved in even the largest of these research efforts was so small as to render the results statistically insignificant.

It was not until December 2006 that two Dutch social scientists—Matthus Kalmijn and Christiaan W. S. Mondon of Tilburg University—published the most large-scale, definitive investigation of the escape hypothesis to be produced thus far. Kalmijn and Mondon (like Waite et al.) analyzed data derived from the National Study of Families and Households—but the questions the Dutch researchers sought to answer were different.

Kalmijn and Mondon wanted to know: Were there more symptomatic aftereffects (e.g., depression, anxiety, substance abuse) in cases where the marriage had been fairly good and ended for relatively trivial reasons, such as "poor communication" or "falling out of love"? And were there fewer symptoms of depression and anxiety when the marriage had been extremely hostile and conflicted—so that the relief of getting out of it served to diminish or counter any bad after-effects? Finally, did the escape hypothesis come into full flower when there had been physical aggression in the marriage?

As Kalmijn and Mondon later reported in the *Journal of Marriage and Family*, they used a well-tested depressive-symptom scale as their central measure of well-being. Thus:

> Respondents reported the number of days during the previous week that they experienced the following: "you were bothered by things that don't usually bother you?," "you felt lonely?," "you felt you could not shake off the blues, even with the help of your family or friends?," "your sleep was restless?," "you felt depressed?," "you felt that everything you did was an effort?," "you felt fearful?," "you had trouble keeping your mind on what you were doing?," "you talked less than usual?," "you did not feel like eating, your appetite was poor?," "you felt sad?," and "you could not get going?"

Participants in the research were also asked about their degree of marital satisfaction on that same 7-point scale ranging from 1, *very unhappy*, to 7, *very happy*, that was used in the Waite analysis. In the Dutch study, the scholars looked at their respondents over a five-plus-year interval, and measured their states of well-being at two successive points in time. Like their American counterparts, Kalmijn and Mondon found that "people who experience a divorce have a significantly greater increase in depressive symptoms between the [initial interview and the interview that occurs years later] . . . than people who remain married."

As far as the escape hypothesis was concerned, Kalmijn and Mondon found scant evidence for its existence in their sizable group of respondents. The scholars did find some evidence that if a person left a bad marriage, the ensuing depressive symptoms were usually not as acute as those of someone who had left a good marriage—but in both cases, some depression was present. No matter what the quality of the former relationship—terrible or not that bad—in the wake of a divorce, both individuals were typically feeling worse than they had earlier.

The most startling result that emerged from this research was that individuals who experienced the steepest decline in well-being after having divorced were those who had been in marriages that involved physical violence. This finding was completely counterintuitive, for people in battering relationships were the very ones to whom the escape hypothesis should most apply. Shouldn't feelings of sheer *relief* counter or totally negate the bad effects of the marital breakup? No; to the scholars' great surprise, the story told by the evidence pointed in the opposite direction. As Professor Mondon told me, this strange finding left him and his coauthor puzzled and unable to explain this unexpected, somewhat bizarre phenomenon. Did it have to do with the fact that when the abuser and the ex-spouse had children in common, it proved impossible to cut off contact completely?

TRAUMATIC BONDING

Still, the investigators remained unsure about how to explain why an ex-partner would feel far *worse* in the aftermath of a relationship in which the other partner had been periodically harassing, intimidating or physically attacking his less-powerful mate. But a phenomenon that psychologists have termed "traumatic bonding" may provide part—or in some instances all—of the explanation.

Traumatically bonded relationships are characterized by what is known as "intermittent reinforcement"—that is, alternating intervals of reward (lovingness and warmth) and punishment (psychological or physical abuse). It has been well established that relationships of this kind—i.e., those that fluctuate between outbursts of belligerence and times of loving tenderness—create emotional attachments that are far *stronger* than attachments that proceed on a steadier, more even keel. The paradoxical truth is that this mode of inconsistent, unpredictable relating creates a glue-like connection between the oppressor and the oppressed, always apprehensive partner. This is why, as painful and damaging as these fear-ridden relationships may be, they are known to be extremely hard to sever.

What gives these relationships their awful power? Therapist and author Janet Geller, Ph.D., who works with couples in physically abusive situations, told me that most individuals living with an assaultive partner can recall an earlier time when the relationship felt safe and secure, and the mate's behavior was far more caring and affectionate. "Things were *good* at one time," Dr. Geller explained, "and maybe they have continued to be good from time to time—especially in the wake of an outburst, when the partners are in the making-up phase."

As this pattern develops, the victimized person becomes accustomed to just hanging on, waiting for the rewarding part to reemerge. She (it is typically a "she") becomes used to trying to get the relationship back to the way it was in the beginning. Her life is always "on hold," and even after she has left the partner, she finds it hard to extricate herself from the relationship in a clear-cut, definitive fashion.

In addition, the fact that the disempowered partner's efforts have been rewarded from time to time have provided her with the long-standing habit of attempting to retrieve the yearned-for *gratifying* parts of the relationship. She has become accustomed to what learning theorists call an "intermittent reinforcement schedule," one that's *kept* her in a state of anxious anticipation throughout the course of the relationship. She has learned to hold fast to the hope that she will get it *right*, eventually—that whatever she does that keeps making her mate surly and aggressive will be clarified and worked out—and that the marriage will proceed much more smoothly in the future. Even after separation and divorce, the alternating hope and despair that have bound her to her abusive mate don't necessarily end with a legal decree.

We know that, being human, the victim feels an instinctive impulse to run for comfort to the person closest to her when she is feeling endangered. But her predicament is complicated by the fact that she is in need of comfort and soothing from the very person who has *caused* the anxiety and trepidation that she (and perhaps her children) have been experiencing.

Furthermore, over the course of time, the abuser has become ever more dominant and empowered as she's become more and more unsure about who she is as a person. Inevitably, the abuse she's absorbed has affected her sense of adequacy, self-worth and basic lovability, while her psychological dependence on her aggressive mate's approval has continued to expand.

This unstable, confusing state of affairs has historically been rendered ever more bewildering by those periodic glimpses of the *good* parts of the relationship—the way things were at the beginning, and the way she thought they would become again one day. This periodic positive reinforcement has served to keep her hopes alive; and, during times when things were going well, she would often indulge in the fantasy that their problems had been resolved and the rewarding parts of the attachment were here to stay.

This fond belief has been bolstered by his changed behavior during the couple's making-up phases, for at these times he will have typically shown some remorse and been more understanding, friendly and affectionate. He has put on his "angel" face, and this calms her; she experiences a huge (if temporary) sense of relief.

It should be understood that these lagoons of relief are not only mental; they exist at a *physical* level as well. For the victim's bodily reaction to her partner's attack has been to switch into an instantaneous readiness (fight, flight or freeze) to meet the threat that confronts her. Her *internal being* is in a highly agitated state of heightened arousal. And in fact, some experts believe that the reason traumatic bonds are far stronger and more difficult to detach than healthier bonds is because they are forged in an atmosphere of such high intensity—an atmosphere in which deep-seated fears and alarms alternate with the release of tension during times of relative tranquillity.

The traumatic bonds that are formed in highly threatening, physically abusive relationships are not dissimilar from other strong emotional attachments formed between a dominant, periodically attacking person and someone who perceives herself or himself to be hopelessly subjugated. The famous Stockholm syndrome was one such instance in which, during the course of their captivity, some female prisoners in Sweden fell in love with the bank robbers who had taken them hostage. Other such intermittently terrifying/loving relationships are those that can spring up between master and slave, or between the maltreated child and his or her tyrannizing parent. In this regard, it is well known that children who have been dreadfully abused by hostile or severely neglectful caretakers still love their parents passionately, and resist being forced to leave their homes.

The abused ex-partner may be in a similar position—highly distressed and yet unable to achieve a clean, ungrieved-for separation from someone who, she well knows, can do nothing other than inflict further harm upon her and perhaps others dear to her too.

Chapter Three

LIZ AND JEFF DENNISON

CLASSMATES

L iz Dennison, age sixty-four, and Jeff Dennison, sixty-eight, had been married for forty-four years at the time of our interviews. When Liz told me that she was nineteen, going on twenty, at the time of their wedding, Jeff laughed and said, "I married a teenager." When he retired, at age sixty, Jeff was a management and marketing consultant, running a small firm of his own.

I was charting an outline of their career and family histories on my sketch pad. Even though I was aware that sixty to sixty-two are the average ages at which Americans now retire, Jeff looked so healthy and vital that it seemed early to me. So I asked him whether, in order to retire in his relatively young years, he had already made his pile and had enough money for them to live on for the rest of their lives.

Jeff, a muscular, trim-looking man, with threads of gray in his brown hair and a barely receding hairline, answered with a shrug. He said that his consulting business had been tapping out at the time of his retirement, and he'd had to make a choice between trying to drum up more business or enjoying his life. "I had made enough, I thought, from then on out. . . . But the problem *now* is that we are going to live forever. And we just don't have enough money for forever."

I glanced at Liz, who looked skeptical but said nothing. She was sitting a few feet from Jeff on the gold tweed sofa in the quiet upstairs sitting room where I conduct interviews in my home. I was seated in a back-friendly maroon-and-gold chair opposite them, and my recorder was on the square coffee table between us.

Although the Dennisons make their home in Cambridge, Massachusetts, they were on one of their periodic visits to their married son Greg and his young family, who live in the New Haven area.

"So your feeling is that you are going to live for a long, long time?" I asked Jeff.

"His dad is ninety-seven." Liz was the one to answer. She is a diminutive, slender woman, with dark chestnut-colored bangs and short, loosely curling hair. "And his mom just died at ninety-three. He has really good genes." As I gazed at the couple, it seemed to me that both Dennisons appeared much younger than their stated ages. It wasn't just a matter of the way they looked; there was something physically vibrant about them. For lack of a better word, I would have said they seemed peppy.

Jeff grinned, and added that he'd had an aunt who died at ninety-eight, another who died at ninety-six and an uncle who died at ninety-one. He laughed. "My grandmother died in an accident at a nursing home at eighty-six. Otherwise she'd still be alive."

"Wow, your family has supped at the Fountain of Longevity." I laughed, too. "And what about *your* family?" I asked Liz.

"My parents are no longer living. And I don't have that fairy-tale attitude that I'm going to live forever. I want to enjoy life *now*, because

I don't have the same sense that it will go on and on until I'm a hundred and ten." She told me that her own dad had died at age sixty-nine and her mother had died at age eighty-eight.

"Eighty-nine," Jeff corrected her.

Her mother had been almost eighty-nine, Liz agreed.

I asked her what her father had died from. At the same time I noted that at the time of her dad's death, at age sixty-nine, he'd been just one year older than Jeff's age at present.

Her father had died from pancreatic cancer.

Had there been other members of her family who'd died of cancer? I asked. Her mother's father had died of stomach cancer.

"Do you ever find yourself thinking about cancer in relation to yourself?" I asked.

Liz shook her head. "No, I really don't think about it. I just don't see an endless future the way Jeff does. I'm more of a realist. I've lost a number of friends who were quite young to heart attacks and other diseases."

"Your brother," her husband prompted.

Liz jumped slightly, as if she'd just been neglectful, then said she'd had a younger brother who had died at age forty-nine. She seemed doubtful about what, exactly, he had died from. "Probably his heart . . . though he'd been ill with schizophrenia most of his life, and I'm sure that contributed to his poor physical state." Her brother, four years younger, had been her only sibling. At sixty-four, Liz was the sole surviving member of her family of origin.

Jeff was an oldest son, with two younger sisters, both married and with families of their own. He described himself as being "in contact," but not particularly close to either one of them. The demanding job of overseeing the care of their elderly parents had fallen largely on his and his wife's shoulders. The couple had also taken over the care of Liz's aging mom until her death from Alzheimer's the previous year.

Given that they had three adult children of their own—and two grandchildren—Jeff thought of himself and his wife as part of the sandwich generation. "For the past five years, we've been dealing with one parent's crisis or another. *Many* hospitalizations. We lost both our mothers within the past two years, and I'm the one who's been handling the financial stuff all along—paying the caregivers; doing all the taxes; arranging all the medical plans, bills and everything else," Jeff said, in a tone that carried no resentment.

Then he went on to say that in their very advanced years, both his parents had become demented. His dad, at ninety-seven, was "in and out of reality"; and in her last years, Liz's mother had been unable to recognize her daughter.

"We've lived through the horror of seeing these three people so changed and alienated from themselves, and it's just *terrible*. My mother was an opinionated, active woman—active in charities, active politically, everything. And she became a little, quiet, smiling, white-haired lady whom nobody even recognized." Jeff shook his head, looking dismayed.

Then he said, his voice sober, that he and Liz had made an informal kind of suicide pact: an agreement that ensured neither of them would have to go on living in this kind of altered, vegetative state. There was something about the way he made this statement that left me feeling, rightly or wrongly, that I should ask nothing more about the details of this arrangement. So I let the subject rest there.

At the same time I reflected that the recent research on heredity and long life, as reported in a current issue of *Human Genetics*, has found that "good genes" account for a *mere 3 percent of the outcome* when it comes to living long or dying young. In a rigorous scientific study comparing the life spans of identical twins and fraternal twins, it was found that the identical twins—who share all their genes and, by the way, the same environment—tended to age differently and, in the majority of cases, die years apart.

Jeff's parents' longevity did not, therefore, necessarily support his conviction that he would "live forever." Nor did it predict with any certainty that his life span would be sure to outstrip his financial resources by so many years that he would become impoverished, as he so clearly feared.

Classmates

It was in the mid-1990s that the Dennisons decided to go back to school. Together, they enrolled in a single undergraduate course at his alma mater, Harvard, whose policy it was to encourage returning students to attend regular classes at a much-reduced fee. "At that time we'd just gotten started with the class when a lot of consulting work came in," Jeff said. "So we had to drop that course. But by the following fall, the consulting business was dying."

"What was making it die?" I asked.

Jeff shrugged, said without animus that he believed it was his age. He went on to say that in the field of marketing and consulting, there is a violent prejudice against age. "Once I began looking older than fifty, it was an uphill battle. The guys who were hiring me as a consultant were fifteen years my junior. They thought that to be au courant with what was happening in the world, you would have to be their age or younger still. And at some point it becomes an uphill battle, one that isn't worth fighting."

I asked him if it had been a bit of a shock to his ego, and he said that it hadn't. "I had ten years of knowing this was coming," Jeff said equably. "In corporate life it's often pocket-wise to replace older workers and start afresh with young, cheap labor. So you can't blame them for doing that because they're being driven by marketplace imperatives."

It surprised me that he didn't seem to be taking this kind of age discrimination personally. Or if he had been outraged eight years before, at the time of his business's demise, the issue seemed to be one that was settled in his mind. A pause ensued, during which I reflected on the series of psychological studies, discussed in the following chapter, which demonstrate that a feature of later adulthood is that people show a marked improvement in the domain of emotional control. I also recalled a conversation with the late Morton Reiser, a psychoanalyst and expert in neuroscience, who told me that as the brain ages, there is a significant loss of neurons in that area called the locus coeruleus. This is a brain structure known to be implicated in states of anger and aggression.

I ended the silence by moving on to more general questions about retirement, and about finding meaningful, purposeful ways to spend time. This was initiated by my asking Liz if she had been a working woman in the years before Jeff's retirement.

She said she'd begun working as a kindergarten teacher before her children were born; and afterward, she'd done some substitute teaching occasionally. For the most part, though, she had been a stay-at-home mom. She had dabbled in several other careers throughout the course of their marriage—catering was one of them—but her last and most satisfying job had been working for her husband's consulting firm.

"We had a real *partnership*, then," she said enthusiastically. "I would do interviews early in the morning, while he slept; and then he would organize the information into a coherent whole in the afternoon, while I slept." They'd been involved in gathering technical information about things such as industrial compressors: attitudes about their client's brand; what customers looked for in the product; how they felt about the pricing; what new features they might be interested in, etc.

Jeff laughed and said that the companies he consulted for inhabited a male-oriented world, so the great advantage of having his wife do the calling was that the men would be disarmed by having a woman talking to them on the phone about all these "guy" kinds of concerns. "It never occurred to them that she could be doing any kind of industrial snooping, which is part of what it was. So it was a great entree for her to get the answers that I could probably not have gotten." He looked at Liz, and the pair exchanged a complicit, affectionate smile.

"So you worked in sync very well until your retirement?" I asked them.

"Right," Jeff replied, but added that since that time the two college courses that they took each semester had become a central focus for them: they'd taken classes in a wide range of subjects, including architecture, history, literature and film studies. "Aside from the family, we have two important things in our lives. We have the courses, and we have travel. Right?" He turned again to his wife.

"Oh, absolutely." She nodded her agreement.

I asked them how much they traveled.

Liz said, "More and more and more. We travel whenever we're out of school. We've been doing the United States, recently . . . trips that vary in length from a week to seven weeks."

Their last trip had taken them to Banff, Vancouver, Victoria and Seattle; then to Portland, down to the Redwoods, and they had returned via Glacier National Park and Yellowstone. "Part of it is camping out," Jeff said. "We have tents, sleeping bags and an ice chest; and we pitch our tent in the national parks and camp out."

"You don't camp out in the snowy ones, do you?" I asked, impressed.

"No, when it snowed . . ." He paused, then said, "Well, actually we went down to thirty degrees," in a proud tone of voice.

"Not by *choice*," Liz put in wryly. "I myself would like a little bit more luxury. But Jeff is still so happy with our original tent . . . even as the netting wears out, the zippers rip, he is *happy* with it." She was laughing.

I smiled, but said nothing. Still, I was aware of feeling a welter of responses. One was admiration: these people managed to enjoy their lives despite the cloud of caregiving worries and responsibilities that had hung over their lives for a substantial part of the past five years. The other was, admittedly, a tinge of jealousy: the Dennisons seemed to have a second wind at their back. They were clearly so adept at making the most of these postretirement years, while I knew that I had not yet faced my own uncertainties about how my husband and I would be able to handle them. Our regular career activities—my writing and his research—were also our main hobbies, and so central to our way of being that I could not envision a life without and beyond them.

I had, however, noticed that while our friends were doing many new things, such as traveling to far-flung destinations like India and China, we had been traveling less than ever. A bout of back trouble (mine) and a hip operation (his) had, I thought, left us feeling cautious.

The Dennisons' descriptions of their trips made me feel winsome, as if my husband and I had to get ourselves up to speed again.

Now Jeff said, as if to counter his wife's remarks about wanting "a little but more luxury," that theirs was an odd kind of camping. They would pitch a tent and sleep in it, then have cold cereal, fruit and yogurt for breakfast. For dinner, however, they would go to the best restaurant in the area. "If there's a great inn nearby, we will go to that; or if we're in a national park, we'll go to the finest lodge."

Liz leaned toward me, said comfortably, "He does a lot of research to find the best places to eat."

"I have a number of websites that I use to search out the places beforehand," Jeff explained. "So we start out with an itinerary, which includes reservations at restaurants, inns and campgrounds."

I looked from one to the other, then said wistfully, "It sounds like you two have a lot of fun together."

"Yeah," Jeff said, "we do."

Liz, smiling, said, "We do," almost simultaneously.

MARITAL HAPPINESS: THE U-SHAPED CURVE

I asked the Dennisons to give me some adjectives that would describe this time of their lives, as compared with when they were in their mid-thirties or early forties.

" 'Tranquil,' is that okay?" Jeff said. I nodded, shrugged my shoulders as if to say there were no right or wrong answers to this question.

"For me . . . I think . . . it's more of a rebirth," Liz said, choosing her words carefully, as if struggling to take hold of her thoughts.

"A rebirth?" I asked.

"It's an *opportunity*. I didn't have a chance to go away to college," she replied. "I went to a city college, and I had to take two buses to get there. So for me to have a chance to be really *reborn* as this privileged Ivy League student . . . to have the incredible opportunity to attend classes taught by these gifted professors—it's just wonderful! It *is* really like being reborn, in a way! And I suppose it's 'tranquil' because we're not dealing with a lot of the problems that these young students have."

"Yes," Jeff said, his voice sober. "We had a lot of trouble with our own kids when they were growing up."

"So you two have had some rocky times along the way?" I asked.

Jeff answered with a quick shrug. "Of *course* there have been some rocky times along the way." But neither of them said anything further.

For a space of time we sat in silence. As we did I thought about the so-called U-shaped curve of marital happiness. Over the past forty years, there have been a number of influential studies showing that a couple's sense of satisfaction and well-being is at its peak during the honeymoon and then begins to erode during the subsequent years. Research shows that this sense of disenchantment is most pronounced during the first few years of married life, and then stabilizes at a less blissful but more realistic level thereafter—unless the relationship breaks apart in this early, most dangerous phase.

For couples who *do* survive these early, perilous years and remain together to raise their young children—and who then survive the stormy challenges of the adolescent years—a movement in a more positive direction predictably occurs. As the parental nest empties, the couple's sense of satisfaction and well-being rises.

During this period of life, the marital U-curve is moving upward on the opposite side. Now each member of the couple has the luxury of thinking about her or his own self—and about the relationship—

and they have the time to focus on their own needs and wishes with a new sense of freedom. The major burdens of parenting are behind them. As I sat with the Dennisons, it seemed to me that they were a fine example of this phenomenon.

At last Jeff spoke up to tell me that their oldest child, a son, had become rebellious and enraged in his late teens. Greg had been so *angry* at them, and so out of control, that they'd had to get involved in a tough love program. "Do you know what that is?" he asked me.

I nodded. I knew that tough love was a behavior modification program for parents of troubled teenagers, one that showed parents how to hold tight and take a firm stand. Basically, it taught members of the senior generation how to change their own behaviors in ways that would bring about positive changes in their kids. "We actually had to resort to something that extreme in order to figure out how to deal with our son," Jeff told me.

To which Liz added, "Greg was just *horrible* until, eventually, he calmed down and got into shape." Now, at thirty-five, their son was happily married, and the father of two daughters, ages eight and four. "We *adore* our little granddaughters," she told me, noting that her son and his family lived in the Lincoln Street area of New Haven, and that she and Jeff drove down to see them often.

Their second child, a daughter, had been economically dependent upon them until she was almost thirty years old. She'd been a medical student, and then a resident in internal medicine; she had earned a Ph.D. in molecular biology simultaneously. Now, at last, she was self-supporting. At thirty-three, she was unmarried, but had been in a long-term relationship with another physician; that relationship had recently ended. Liz and Jeff were in close contact with this middle child also.

But their youngest child, now thirty years old, had set up some distance between herself, her parents and her older siblings. They spoke to her less often, and didn't know a great deal about what was going on in her life. "Jenny is a very private person. I know that she would like to be seeing someone, but her weight has been an issue. She's quite overweight, and doesn't feel good about herself." Liz's voice had dropped, as if she felt shame or grief on behalf of her daughter.

Jenny was the shortest member of the family and was carrying about thirty-five pounds of extra weight, her father said. Although they talked on the phone with her much less often than they did with their other kids—and Jenny controlled the timing of the calls—they always spoke warmly and for a long time whenever they were in contact. Jenny was an attorney, working in Washington, D.C.

I asked the Dennisons whether there was more that they wanted to say about their adult children before our interview moved on.

" 'Adult children.' " Liz repeated my phrase as though turning it over in her mind. "That has a nice . . ." She didn't complete her thought, but her cheeks reddened suddenly, and she said in a rush, "Oh, I *wish* my daughters would get married! I would love to have some sons-in-law! I would love to have more grandchildren, more of an expanded family! I think when I lost my brother and my parents—and especially having just lost my mother—my whole connection to the past was just snipped off. I was just set loose, and what I want, more and more, is to send out new roots."

I turned to Jeff, asked him if he felt the same way. He shrugged, said that he would like to see his girls settled but didn't feel as deeply about it as Liz did. "I would like to see them married because I think they would be happier married than not. I would like to see them have kids, because what's the point of a family if you don't have kids?"

His was the solid voice of reason in regard to situations that were realistically not under their control.

COMPROMISE

In response to the question *What are the ways in which you have disappointed and surprised each other, over time?* Jeff Dennison drew a blank. He couldn't think of a way in which his wife had disappointed him.

"You're not disappointed that I don't love camping as much as you do?" Liz inquired teasingly.

Jeff answered by addressing me: "I've found through experience that if I'm just persistent, sooner or later Liz will give in. . . . So that when I face a situation where I want to go camping and she doesn't . . ." He stopped.

"You go camping." I finished his sentence with a smile.

He shrugged and smiled, too. "And she'll come along. When I say I'm going, she'll come along."

Liz, defending him or herself, said that they *did* compromise occasionally. Jeff agreed to stay at motels periodically where they could get a hot shower and a comfortable bed.

"Right," Jeff said, but added that he still could not think of any ways in which she'd disappointed him.

I recalled something Liz had said earlier in the interviews: she had described herself as a very conforming, docile, good child who'd listened to her parents and hadn't rebelled in any way. She had been very interested in biology and had wanted to be a doctor, but her parents believed that the only "female" professions possible were that of teacher, nurse or dietitian. So her range of career choices had been very limited.

It seemed to me that her life options must have been even more hemmed in by the existence of her schizophrenic brother. To the growing girl, it was probably self-evident that she had to be dependably "good" and not a source of added stress to her parents, who already had far too much to handle.

Liz believed now that she should have been more insistent at that time—more oriented toward her own personal goals, more self-fulfilling.

"That wasn't your style, though," I'd suggested. "You weren't a fighter."

"It's not my style," Liz had said.

I asked both Dennisons, "You're not a conflictual couple at all, are you?" To which Liz answered, her expression contented, "No, I think we've been lucky in that I usually do give in, so that we don't have a battle."

My eyebrows shot up, and Jeff said hurriedly, "We have our conflicts, but they get resolved."

"I think we compromise," Liz said, revising her own statement and looking not at all disturbed or disgruntled.

PORNOGRAPHY

It was late in the interview when I asked the Dennisons, *What do you think are the major sexual issues that emerge at this time of life?*

There was a long pause before Jeff said, "For a man, I guess it's performance anxiety. And while I don't have that now, I did go through a brief period of performance anxiety . . . and then it passed." During his period of sexual uncertainty, he said, he tried "the little blue pill, Viagra. But now I haven't used it in a year. . . . I found it doesn't do any

more for me than Mother Nature, and Mother Nature is okay. I think
the pill has an effect, but it's not enough of an effect to be worth eight
dollars."

"Eight dollars?" I asked.

"Yes, that's what a pill costs, and I asked myself, 'Am I getting eight
dollars' worth out of this?' "

"How about you?" I asked, turning to Liz.

She shrugged. "Of course there are hormonal changes. Vaginal thinning and all that stuff. So I take hormone replacements, both pills:
low dosages of estrogen and a vaginal estrogen replacement called
Vagifem."

"I guess I forget about that part, *her* part, but I probably shouldn't.
I mean, that is my woman and I'm going to have sex with her,"
Jeff said.

"I do weight lifting, and that cuts back on the hormones," Liz continued, "but I no longer have the desire of a woman in her twenties."

"Yes," I said, encouraging her to continue.

"Still, I do think—" she started to say, but Jeff interrupted: "Just to
put this in perspective, I still feel the same kind of sexual interest in
her as I have for the last fifteen years."

"And that's certainly one of the problems we've had to deal with,"
Liz said. I took this to mean a difference in their levels of sexual
desire. But I was mistaken.

For Liz went on to say, "Because there he was, and there was all this
pornography on the Internet . . . and he was getting on these chat
rooms at night . . ."

I paused, surprised. Jeff looked startled, as surprised by her revelation as I was. He gave me a long look, shrugged slightly, then said,
"Yeah, I guess I'll talk to you about it. We discovered the Internet and

we discovered all this free porn, and it becomes something you gotta do, gotta do, gotta do, and then . . ."

I waited for him to continue. He was using the editorial "we," when he really meant "I," and the repetition of "gotta do" made me wonder whether he was addicted.

"But not just that—" Liz started to say.

"Then I began cutting back on it at the same time you finally became accepting of it," Jeff said to her directly. "You viewed it in the sense of 'Oh, this is a guy thing, just let him do it and get over it.' It was the right way to handle it, finally."

"But it was very difficult for me," Liz said. "Because it felt very *personal*. Like I was no longer . . . the one." She was addressing me. "There were all these other women who were talking with him in a sexy way, and I would just go to sleep by myself. He would be in there with these other ladies, and it was very *hard* for me."

I nodded sympathetically, for as I pictured the situation it sounded *very* personal and somehow weird to me—out of character for this satisfied-seeming pair. At the same time I knew that the Internet is awash in pornography, and that a great many "nice guys" like Jeff Dennison—and "nice women" as well—get involved in it, with varying outcomes in regard to whether they eventually meet face-to-face or do not.

Jeff said he first went online about six years ago. "But on the Net I wasn't sixty years old, I was in my late forties. Just the age they wanted me to be . . . old enough to have experience, maturity, wisdom." He laughed at the memory; his sense of embarrassment had faded. It sounded as if it had been a sexy game for him, in which he assumed the false identity of a strapping forty-something-year-old man, not the real sixty-year-old man he actually was.

"I'll bet a lot of the women were lying about *their* ages, too," I observed dryly.

He nodded. "Probably." But over time, he said, Liz had become more "accepting" and "mature" about his Internet activities. She had stopped paying attention to them, and eventually he himself became somewhat weary of the whole thing. "The women at the other end probably thought they had discovered a gold mine, because I could ask good questions; I could give understanding responses and ideas; and it must have been terrific for them." I smiled; his voice held a note of braggadocio.

It had been diverting and enjoyable for a while when he was turning sixty, Jeff continued, but then he began to tire of it. "I was on the Net pretty regularly for a couple of years, but after a while it just felt like the same old, same old. It wasn't really physical sex; it was mental sex. And while a lot of sex *is* mental, this was *all* mental. And you know, sex has to be physical as well as mental. . . . So you become jaded after a while. I haven't done . . . God, it's been *years* since I've been online. Some of these women might come back on the screen once in a while and say, 'Hey, I haven't seen you for such a long time!' but . . ." He stopped, shrugged to say he had lost all interest.

I nodded. Just losing interest was, I thought, the difference between a genuine pornography addict and a guy who'd become fascinated by this novel, risk-free mode of sexual adventuring for a while.

I asked Jeff if his Internet correspondents ever sent pictures of themselves to him.

"Very occasionally, but you know you can't trust them anyway," he replied, with an indifferent lift of his shoulders. So he had lied about who he was—a stud of forty, not a gentleman of sixty—while assuming that the women with whom he was having these torrid exchanges were lying about who *they* were, as well! There was a sense in which it was all a big joke. The whole thing had the air of a playtime activity, an adult version of a childish "dirty" game like spin the bottle.

True, this revelation had struck me as peculiar, but it became less and less so the more I thought about it. Certainly, it was a discordant part of the overall narrative of the Dennisons' long and presently gratifying relationship. But there are probably such discordant notes in *most* of our lives—matters that we'd be happy to put aside and not talk about with outsiders or, for the most part, with one another.

Moreover, in a long marriage such as Liz and Jeff's, a certain need for a private space—and some restlessness and curiosity about what lies outside the bounds of the relationship—is likely to emerge in one partner or the other. Add to this Liz's remark that her feelings of desire were no longer the same as they had been earlier in the marriage, and it's easy to comprehend why her husband might have gone roaming. But in this instance, Jeff's ranging from the relationship had been minimal, and he had surely kept a sturdy leash on his behavior. For the bottom line was that while his Internet shenanigans might have been hurtful to his wife temporarily, nobody had been seriously harmed.

No other woman had been involved in reality—it had all been a kind of fantasy game—and nobody had been humiliated openly or devastated. Now the Dennisons' marriage was in a period of "tranquillity," and they were having a good deal of fun. Would these long-term partners have handled the whole issue of Internet sex so capably at an earlier phase of their relationship? This was something I couldn't help wondering.

Chapter Four

TAKING TIME SERIOUSLY

I n our youth-intoxicated society, it is obvious that negative attitudes about aging abound. For instance, commonplace beliefs about the older person are that he is someone who is slowed down, uninteresting, intellectually apathetic, rigid in his ways and someone to be dodged—a stereotypical "geezer," in other words.

In the past few decades, social psychologists have been looking closely at these widely held beliefs, some of which are disavowed by many people at an explicit, or conscious, level. A pioneer in this work is Dr. Mahzarin Banaji of Harvard, who has been working with a fascinating research tool called the Implicit Attitudes Test.

The IAT is a kind of "quiz" that ferrets out people's unconscious attitudes toward older people—or some other societally devalued group, such as the poor, blacks, females and so forth—through sophisticated methods using test takers' response times to stimuli (words such as "good-bad," "old-young," etc.). What has been most startling about her findings, Professor Banaji told me in the course of a long interview, is that it is not only the young who hold negative attitudes about older adults; apparently, the majority of older people do, too!

In addition, numerous research studies have described the declining powers that frequently accompany the aging process—such as vision and hearing deficits, slower reaction times, diminished energy and so forth. There has also been much experimental work on the losses in cognitive capacities that are associated with later adulthood: changes in the rapidity of information processing; in working memory (the short-term retention of new information); in reaction timing; in mental imagery; and in problem-solving—these have all been studied in great detail. So have the oft-seen sensory losses: in vision, hearing, and in some instances even taste and smell.

Given all this bad news, what can explain the persistently *good* news, which is known as "the paradox of aging"? This paradox, mentioned earlier, is the consistent finding that, despite the negative social climate in which many older adults exist, and the diminishment of certain capacities, the majority of older adults enjoy a subjective sense of well-being. For example, an analysis of longitudinal data (1971–74) from more than thirty-two thousand Americans—data culled from a huge study carried out by the MacArthur Foundation—disclosed that the majority of older respondents viewed themselves as "very" or "pretty" happy.

And in a 2005 article entitled "Hope I Die Before I Get Old: Mispredicting Happiness Across the Life Span," Dr. Heather Pond Lacey et al. stated that: "People seem to dread growing old, despite *evidence that well-being improves with age.*" Lastly, in the book *Ageism*, researchers Ed Diener and Eunkook M. Suh observed that "findings from around the world support this positive image of aging as a time of increased feelings of satisfaction."

A recent (2006) explanation of this age-related sense of well-being is that it is biological in origin. In an article published in the *Journal of Neuroscience* by Dr. Leanne M. Williams and her colleagues at the University of Sydney in Australia, the researchers reported that "positive changes with age have now been identified as having a neural basis. . . . Specifically, emotional stability has been found to improve linearly from 12 to 79 years of age." Using functional magnetic resonance imaging (FMRI) and measurement of event-related potentials (ERP), these brain scientists determined that across the life course plasticity in the medial prefrontal brain systems increases. "This increase is predicted by changes in the medial prefrontal cortex, changes that allow greater selective control over negative emotions," the researchers determined.

Yet another explanation of the paradox of aging, one that is eminently congruent with the work described above, is provided by a fascinating discovery that has emerged from psychological research carried out during the past decade and a half. Which is that, despite declines in a number of areas of cognitive functioning, there is one important domain—*the emotional domain*—in which older adults experience no downturn at all. Emotionally, individuals in later adulthood are as well-off as they ever were, and frequently even better off, for they often show appreciable gain in terms of emotional regulation. The results of a variety of studies have shown that most older adults have a good opinion of themselves and a positive sense of this period of their lives.

A sense of time is the relevant factor here. According to Professor Laura Carstensen, who is director of Stanford University's Life-span Development Laboratory as well as founding director of the Center on Longevity at Stanford, we humans are all "time travelers." At birth we possess a kind of internal clock, one that starts ticking when we come into the world and continuously monitors where we are in the course of our life span. At every epoch of our lives we possess an internal awareness of how much of our time on earth has transpired, and where we are in terms of life left to live.

In early adulthood, the horizon of time feels as if it were limitless and stretched far into a seemingly boundless future. These are the years of striving to carve out a place in the social world—of the search for love, for success, for perfect happiness at some rosy point in the future. For this reason we may defer emotional gratification in the present—for example, by spending time with people who can enhance our future prospects rather than with those whose company we truly enjoy. These are the years during which we make our place in the world and during which we experience the anxieties, disappointments and setbacks that are inevitably met with over the course of time. It has to be mentioned that as much as we, as a society, admire and extol the years of early adulthood, research studies have consistently demonstrated that younger adults are *not* as happy as adults in their older years.

In the years of later, relatively healthy adulthood (fifty to seventy-five), the horizon of time has shifted and the outlines of a person's life story have become much clearer. In the psychological vocabulary of older adults, the future tense is greatly diminished in importance, and it is the present tense—the possibilities for pleasure, connectedness and a sense of emotional embeddedness—that emerge into prominence.

This has been well described and, as we'll see, well researched by psychologist Carstensen and her Stanford University colleagues. In an important article called "Taking Time Seriously," they write: "People are always aware of time—not only of clock and calendar time, but of lifetime. . . . [W]hen endings are primed people focus on the present rather than the future or the past, and this temporal shift leads to an emphasis on the intuitive and subjective . . . [and] increases the value people place on life and emotion, importantly influencing the decisions they make." In other words, developmentally speaking, older adults tend to live *in the moment*, and this appears to increase their sense of satisfaction and well-being.

It is this sense of time as a precious, diminishing resource that (so the thinking goes) lies at the source of the contentment, pleasure and satisfaction I encountered in so many of the over-fifty partners I interviewed. These couples were at a stage of living during which the existence of the self and of the partner felt inordinately invaluable, to some degree because there was an underlying drumming that was sounding the beat of time's relentless passage. As coresearchers Carstensen, Helene Fung and Susan Charles write: "Essentially, when concerns for the future are less relevant, attention to current feeling-states heightens. Appreciation for the fragility and value of human life increases and long-term relationships with family and friends assume unmatched importance."

PROACTIVE PRUNING

One of the most reliable findings in social gerontology is that as people age, their social circles begin to shrink. Why does this happen? For decades one of the most accepted theoretical explanations was that of "disengagement." The idea was that in their declining years, people begin to withdraw, for their friends die or move away, and they feel "devitalized," with little to offer in relationships with new or old associates. As time passes, their emotional affect becomes ever flatter and they slowly disengage from their social connections in a gradual preparation for death.

But this theory has languished in the aftermath of population-based studies, which show that older adults are in fact *less* anxious and depressed than younger people. And, as noted earlier, national and international studies have shown that the majority of people in their later years are actually pretty satisfied with their lives and have a sense of well-being. Younger adults are—despite their lack of wrinkles—more dissatisfied with their close relationships than are their elders, who feel stronger bonds to time-tested old friends and increasing intimacy with members of their families as well.

So what can explain the shrinking of older adults' social circles? According to Carstensen, it has to do with what she terms "proactive pruning." As Carstensen explains, we all experience a sense of the expansiveness of time when we are in our younger years, and of how foreshortened time's horizon becomes in later adulthood. In our older years, the here and now is *what we have;* and so, under conscious or unconscious influences, we begin behaving in ways that will increase the positive nature—or what she calls the "positivity"—of our interactions with those around us. That is, we act in ways that will render our relations with family members and close friends as satisfying as possible.

Because of this, new acquaintances are of diminishing importance to us—we'll have less time to forge a real connection to them—and at the same time, we go about pruning the toxic people from our lives. In this phase of life, our emphasis is on increasing closeness to the smaller circle of intimates who are dear to us, time-tested and truly do matter. Now the emotionally meaningful aspects of our lives are of utmost importance, for they are being lived under time's internally monitored constraints.

A THEORY OF SOCIOEMOTIONAL SELECTIVITY

Proactive pruning is but one aspect of socioemotional selectivity theory (SST), which has been developed over the past decade and a half at the Life-span Development Laboratory at Stanford University. Admittedly, the term is a ponderous one, but this theoretical approach has been validated by a variety of studies (several of which I describe below).

The central tenet of socioemotional selectivity theory is that the *appraisal of time* plays a critical role in the ranking of differing types of goals and the choices we make in order to attain them. Thus, in early and middle adulthood, we tend to give preference to instrumental— knowledge and information-related—goals that will further our way in the world, and we strive actively to achieve them. The time left for living feels so ample that emotional fulfillment can be put on hold until some date in the distant and amorphous future. But socioemotional selectivity theory posits that this motivational tendency shifts with increasing age, and with the ever-growing appreciation that time has become a diminishing resource.

The awareness that the clock of life is ticking and that time is, in some sense, running out initiates a realignment of our motivational goals and, therefore, of the aging person's subsequent behavior. For later adulthood brings with it the realization that we can maximize the positive, pleasurable aspects of our lives by spending more time with those with whom we have established close, benign relationships, rather than wasting our energy on unproven or unrewarding social acquaintances. New acquaintances are less attractive than comfortable old friends and beloved family members, and those individuals with whom we have had hurtful relationships are held at a greater distance. In brief, novelty and information seeking take second place to the here and now of present-day emotional fulfillment. Now the most important goals revolve around enjoying the emotional gratification that can be realized in the immediacy of everyday existence.

AGING AND THE POSITIVITY EFFECT

One of the most surprising findings in social psychology has been the discovery that while the aging mind experiences an inevitable decline in a range of cognitive capacities, the domain of emotional functioning is not only spared but actually improves. A series of experiments carried out by the life-span researchers at Stanford, and in other laboratories as well, has documented the fact that older adults pay more attention to positive than negative information. For example: in one study older and younger adults were asked to view a computer screen in which one emotional face (showing either positive or negative affect, such as joy or sadness) appeared side by side with one neutral face for a brief, single second.

When the two faces faded from sight after the second had expired, a dot appeared where one of the faces had been—either the emotional face or the neutral one. The subjects were then asked to recall which face the dot had replaced—the face showing happy, unhappy or no affect at all. When the results of this study were examined, a clear difference between the older and the younger participants emerged.

The older subjects were much *faster* to respond to the faces with positive expressions than to those with negative or neutral expressions. The younger people, on the other hand, showed no pronounced differences in their responses to the positive, negative or neutral faces. Those in their later adult years were evidently oriented toward retaining in memory an image with a positive valence.

This kind of "positivity effect" has been demonstrated over and over again in a variety of different studies carried out over the past fifteen years. Age differences can be found not only in memory for emotional faces but for photographs, words and in slide shows. As researchers Mara Mather and Laura Carstensen observe, "these positivity effects . . . [have been found to be] . . . consistent across men and women, African and European-Americans, and people of high and low socioeconomic status." In one Life-span Laboratory study, carried out by developmental researchers Mikel et al., it was even found that older adults *outperformed* younger adults on a working memory task—i.e., one that involved recall of recently learned information—if the task involved positive stimuli. This finding is a curious one, given that it is known that working memory diminishes in effectiveness as we age.

In the same study it was shown that younger adults showed superior memory performance when the task involved stimuli that were negative in nature. But this is no surprise, because it has been well documented that younger people often attend to negative stimuli preferentially. They are motivated toward focusing on the threats and challenges that may arise in the future.

TRACKING EMOTIONS IN DAILY LIFE

An intriguing study of the everyday ups and downs experienced by adults of differing ages was carried out by Carstensen and colleagues in the late 1990s. The purpose of this work was to assess the frequency, intensity and complexity of people's emotional experiences as they went about the ordinary activities of their lives.

The subjects taking part in the study consisted of a racially and socioeconomically diverse sample comprising 184 individuals ranging in age from eighteen to ninety-four. Each person was provided with an electronic pager and shown how to use it. Then, for a one-week period, they were paged at random intervals five times during the day. Each time a participant was signaled, he or she would write down the emotion being experienced at that time, and would also give a numerical rating to the feeling's intensity. The list below contains the positive or negative emotions the subject was asked to select from at the moment the pager went off:

NEGATIVE EMOTIONS	POSITIVE EMOTIONS
Anger	Happiness
Sadness	Joy
Fear	Contentment
Disgust	Excitement
Guilt	Pride
Embarrassment	Accomplishment
Shame	Interest
Anxiety	Amusement
Irritation	
Frustration	
Boredom	

At the end of the day, each subject would send a completed response sheet to the Life-span Laboratory in a pre-addressed, stamped envelope. Overall, the 184 people taking part in the study were paged thirty-five times during the experimental week, and each participant sent in a daily report detailing the nature and the strength of his or her ordinary emotional experiences.

When the week ended, and the voluminous data that had been gathered was aggregated and analyzed, this study of adults who were of widely varying ages and who came from a range of diverse backgrounds yielded the following results:

1. *Negative* emotional experiences were quite *high* among younger people, but they showed a steady, sharp decline in frequency across the adult life span. This downtrend was closely tied to the aging process, and continued until around the age of sixty. At that point, negative emotional experiences in daily life seemed to rise somewhat—but they still remained far, far below the level of negativity experienced in the early years of the adult life span.

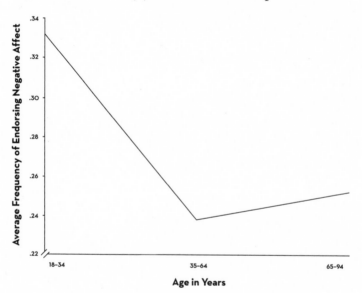

Frequency of Negative Affect Across the Life Span

2. Both younger and older adults experienced *positive* emotional experiences with the same frequency and intensity. However, an important difference between the two groups emerged from this work: when subjects in their older adult years had highly positive

emotional experiences, the "positivity" tended to endure. That is, if an older subject was paged on one sampling, and his or her responses were markedly positive, that person was highly likely to be equally upbeat on the subsequent sampling. This was not the case for younger adult participants in the study.

3. When older adults were reporting highly *negative* experiences, their negativity tended to be more transitory—often, the downbeat nature of their responses had evaporated by the time they were sampled again. This was not true for younger adult subjects, who reported far more negative emotional experiences and whose negative experiences tended to linger.

To everyone's surprise, this study—which was titled "Emotional Experience in Everyday Life Across the Adult Life Span"—produced results that ran counter to our most firmly held societal beliefs. It was *not* the case that people in the glorious, healthy, highly energetic years of their young adulthood experienced many more positive emotions in their daily lives than did those in their later years. On the contrary, not only did older adults appear to have an equal number of positive emotions; they were also able to hold on to their highly positive emotional experiences for longer periods of time, and to let go of their highly negative experiences more readily. The unanticipated reality is that older adults are happier and more optimistic than are those in their younger adult years.

A Changing Emotional Climate

To summarize: in the afternoon of life, as people become aware (consciously or subconsciously) that their time left to live may be unknown, but is certainly limited, they move from a focus on instrumental goals that will pay off at some time in the future to a focus on present-oriented goals that involve feeling-states in the here and now.

An interesting addendum to this work are recent findings which indicate that older people experience relatively *low* rates of psychological disturbance. These findings support the growing evidence that emotional functioning does *not* decline with age, as had previously been supposed. On the contrary, it is a domain that is not only well preserved but often shows improvement with the passage of time.

How does this oft-enhanced state of individual well-being affect the marital life of older people? Psychologist Robert Levenson of the University of California, who has carried out many studies of couples at different stages of the life cycle, says that "the literature certainly suggests that the emotional climate of marriage changes across adulthood."

In my own interviews with married partners, I found that the atmospherics were generally benign. I also discerned repeating themes and issues, many of which revolved around shifts in motivation that are characteristic of later adult development. Eventually, when I began to write about what I was perceiving, the couples I chose to describe in detail were those whose core concerns seemed representative of most of my other interviewees.

For example, in the case of the McBrides, Carl had been emotionally unavailable in his earlier adult years, concerned first and foremost with himself and his career as a musician and an academic administrator. Lynn had felt he made no room for her in their arid, distant relationship, and she'd said she was determined to leave him when their children were grown and had left home.

But the couple's later adulthood brought about enormous changes in Carl's outlook and his goals; and Lynn had been able to recognize and value these changes, and to connect with him in another, far more emotionally real and gratifying way. The McBrides' later adult years had brought to them the awareness that they could have a better, more rewarding relationship by focusing their energies on those close, trusting ways of connecting to each other that had been absent from their marriage earlier in time. And toward the close of our first interview, Lynn had told me, with a smile and a quick glance at her husband, that she had given up the notion of ever leaving Carl and a bond that, in their later years, she had come to treasure.

In a similar vein, Jeff Dennison made a clear-cut choice to enjoy the years of his life that were left to him. His decision had been to retire in his early sixties. "I had made enough, I thought, from then on out. . . . But the problem *now*," he'd said with a laugh, "is that we are going to live forever. And we just don't have enough money for forever." (Remember, Jeff's growing concern was due to his parents' and other blood relatives' unusual longevity.)

Still, he and Liz were clearly relishing this time of their lives together. They were basking in their love of learning by taking a wide range of classes at Jeff's alma mater, and by taking long, adventurous camping trips. At the same time they were honoring their filial role by keeping in daily cell-phone touch with Jeff's ninety-seven-year-old dad, who lived in Florida with a companion/caretaker.

For these partners—and this was true for practically all of the over-fifty pairs I interviewed—it was vitally important to focus *on what and who really mattered* in the world of right now. For this reason, intimate partners in their late adulthood gave clear preference to time-tested, close relationships—primarily those with their grown children, good friends, relatives and other familiar, rewarding connections. Many couples reported that their social circles had indeed contracted, but that the quality of their lives—and especially of their interactions with each other—had shown dramatic improvement.

CLOSELY OBSERVED OLDER COUPLES

Beginning in the 1990s and continuing throughout the subsequent decade, a group of research psychologists began studying the experiences of older, married adults as they interacted with each other under carefully regulated laboratory conditions. Their subjects included couples who were in that stage of healthy later adulthood (fifty-plus) that had been almost nonexistent at the outset of the twentieth century, when the average life expectancy was just 47.6 years.

The core researchers involved in this work were Dr. Robert Levenson, Dr. Laura Carstensen and Dr. John Gottman of Washington State University, who was renowned for his experimental studies of younger pairs in relatively new marriages. Gottman's laboratory observations, begun in the 1970s, had produced consistent results in more than fifty studies carried out in the United States and in other countries around the globe. His studies addressed, among other questions, the fundamental issue of how happily married and unhappily married couples *differed* when it came to resolving their conflicts.

But the subjects taking part in Gottman's studies were all in their twenties (the maximum age of those in the sample was thirty) and they had not been married very long. Given that the average age of the U.S. population was almost forty-five—and on the rise—Levenson, Carstensen and Gottman got together and decided that the next logical step should be a study involving (and comparing) both middle-aged couples and couples in later adulthood.

The psychologists then set about recruiting a large number of marriage partners by means of newspaper, radio, bulletin boards, placards on city buses, etc. Eventually, they winnowed out their sample of 156 couples from a much more extensive group of volunteers. After that, the psychologists subdivided their ethnically and socioeconomically diverse participants into four groups:

1. Happily married middle-aged partners
2. Maritally dissatisfied middle-aged partners
3. Happily married older partners, and
4. Maritally dissatisfied older partners.

The participants in the research were then studied by means of an ingenious procedure developed by Levenson and Gottman in the 1980s. The members of the couple came to the laboratory after not having spoken to each other for the previous eight hours. They were hooked up to recording devices that would register their physiological responses—e.g., heart rate, blood pressure, etc.—on a continuous basis. The marital partners then engaged in three conversations.

The first was a discussion of the events of the day.
The second was an area of continuing disagreement in their
    marriage.
The third was a mutually agreed-upon pleasant topic.

(Actually, the subject of the second discussion—the couple's major conflict—had also been decided upon in advance, in collaboration with a trained interviewer.)

Each conversation lasted for fifteen minutes, preceded by a five-minute silent period. A split-screen video recording was made of the entire session. In the following couple of days the members of the pair returned to the laboratory—separately—on two different occasions. There, they watched the video recording of the three dialogues and provided a continuous report of their (recalled) subjective feelings as they watched the tape. This was accomplished using a rating dial, which was anchored by "extremely negative" at one end and "extremely positive" at the other.

Finally, ratings of the severity of the couple's conflict and the degree of their enjoyment of pleasant events were analyzed and scored in such a way that they could be quantified—that is, recorded as numerical data rather than as words (such as "interest," "affection," etc., or "disgust," "defensiveness," "sadness" and so forth). At the same time, physiological activity (heart rate, galvanic skin response, etc.) was assessed.

The results of this extraordinary experiment were fascinating: the older couples' conflicts were unmistakably less acute than were the middle-aged couples' conflicts. Also, the particular *areas* of disagreement of the midlife group and those in later adulthood tended to differ sharply. Middle-aged couples argued more about children, money, religion and recreation than older couples did. None of the areas of conflict assessed by the researchers was found to be more full of conflict for the older than the younger group.

Furthermore, couples in later adulthood derived more pleasure than did the midlife couples from talking about children and grandchildren, doing things together, dreams and vacations. But *none* of the pleasant topics assessed was more enjoyable for the younger than the older group. "Thus it appears," wrote researchers Levenson, Carstensen and Gottman, "that older couples not only experience less conflict in their marriages, they also experience more pleasure."

To add to this relatively glowing picture of later-life marriage, the scientists found evidence for improved emotion regulation in their observational data. "Older couples, compared to middle-aged couples, expressed lower levels of anger, disgust, belligerence and whining and higher levels of one important emotion, namely *affection*," they observed. It was even found that the "unhappily married" older couples showed affection to each other in the midst of all their complaints and disagreements. These findings proved consistent with an earlier longitudinal study of marriage carried out by Rosalie Gilford and Vern Bengtson in the late 1970s. These researchers also found evidence that relationships improved and couples argued less as they moved into their later adult years.

And obviously the results of this research accord well with Carstensen's life-span theory, which contends that the motivation to regulate emotion and to seek affectively meaningful experience increases as people begin to realize (above or below the water level of consciousness) that their time left on earth is growing shorter. The sun is drifting lower on their life's horizon, and they want this period of their lives to be as rewarding as it can possibly be.

The three authors of this ambitious study observe that

> Emotionally close relationships offer many benefits to older adults. Intimate emotional relationships in later life appear to buffer individuals from mental and physical health problems. The closeness and predictability of long-term relationships provide an important context for achieving emotionally meaningful experience. It may be within this context that, ideally, people master an art of emotion regulation in which understanding a loved one's emotions and even soothing that person's emotions can occur simultaneously with the regulation of one's own emotional state.

Clearly, in learning how to understand and soothe the loved Other, one becomes able to learn more about regulating and soothing the Self.

Chapter Five

JEAN AND NED DONALDSON

THE SIMPLE LIFE

f you look back on your life, what is the thing you are most proud of?

We were nearing the close of a long interview when I put that question to Jean Brenner Donaldson. She didn't hesitate before responding, "My courage, I think."

"Your courage . . . ?" I waited for her to continue.

"Yes," she said. "Yes."

"You mean your courage about making this relationship happen?" I asked, glancing at her husband, Ned, who was leaning forward, elbows on knees, listening to his wife intently. I had already heard the story of her leaving her wealthy physician husband after falling in love with Ned, who was a divorced high school English teacher at that time, making an unimpressive salary and also responsible for alimony and child support.

"Yes, that . . . and everything else that needed to happen," Jean said. "When I needed to be courageous, I reached inside and . . . I *was* courageous." There was fervor in her warm, clear voice and in her velvety brown-eyed gaze.

"What other times were you courageous?" I asked.

Eyeing me thoughtfully, she said, "Oh, picking up and moving to a tiny town in New Hampshire from the suburban world of Fairfield, Connecticut. . . . That meant leaving a whole life behind. Marrying a man who wasn't Jewish . . . going back to graduate school when I had a little baby and I was working. I think the things that have borne the most fruit in my life came out of . . ." She lifted her shoulders lightly.

"Courage." I completed her sentence.

"Courage." Jean nodded her agreement.

KISMET

When they'd first gotten to know each other, as fellow members of a Westchester choral society, Ned was a divorced father in his late thirties, and he was on the prowl. He'd become sexually involved with various female singers in the group, but his relationship with Jean Brenner was completely different. "At that point in my life I was relieved to find that my *best*, my very dearest friend was someone that I didn't have to worry about as a girlfriend. I didn't have to perform for her sexually, because she was married. And it was terrific!"

I smiled. "She was safe." But I wondered if "performance" was an issue for Ned.

"She was *safe*, and we just had the most wonderful times together. It hadn't really entered my mind that anything else was possible." Ned, who is a man of medium height and solidly built, has blue eyes as bright and clear as a Dutch tile. He laughed suddenly, as if surprised anew by the turn their lives had taken.

I turned to Jean. "How about you?"

She smiled a droll smile. "We were on a very different page."

Although they had never become involved in a sexual affair before her marriage ended, Jean said that falling in love with Ned had been the most rebellious act of her entire life. "But it was just . . . *kismet*. It wasn't something you could push aside."

For Jean, it had been a sign—a first sign—that there were forces way over her head, forces beyond her comprehension. She had a sense of being guided by something different, a sense of propulsion forward that was much larger than herself. "It was like a universal love, a huge energy, *God*—I have no trouble calling it God! I'd met this man, and he called up in me a kind of father energy—he was the same sort of gentle, loving, nurturing person. And I wasn't in that kind of marriage," she added dryly.

When she first became friends with Ned, she said, she'd had no idea what she was getting into, except that there *was* an attraction. "It was here," Jean said, pointing to her heart. At some level, ending her marriage and marrying Ned had felt as formidable as trying to move heaven and earth. "But never did they move so easily. When things are *right*, they just happen in the right way."

She and Ned had acknowledged their growing, deepening mutual attraction—but they did not become involved in an affair. At the time, Jean went to her husband and told him that she believed she was falling in love with another man. She found him curiously unperturbed. "It was actually quite a surprise to me, and to everybody, that Larry didn't say, 'Let's go to counseling,' or 'Can't we work on this marriage?' but he wasn't bothered or indignant or anything like that."

"Still, it wasn't easy," Ned reminded her. "You went to him and you said, 'I'm falling in love with this guy, so *do* something! Do something to save this marriage!' And he just . . ." Ned shrugged, as if to say nothing had then happened.

Jean now believed that her ex-husband had been glad, not at all despondent, to hear the news of this situation, for it enabled him to leave the marriage without being the instigator himself. "I was the one who split the family, I was the home wrecker," she said. It was not until two years later, a couple of months before her divorce became final, that she learned that Larry had been involved in a long affair with one of his nurses throughout this entire period. And before that affair, her husband had been involved with someone else. A medical colleague of his, someone who'd remained a mutual friend, had revealed these things to her. "This fellow said he just couldn't *stand* watching me punish myself and drive myself crazy over the breakup of the family, because it wasn't completely my fault." A rosy flush— anger? embarrassment? shame?—rose slowly in her cheeks.

MOVING NORTH

The Donaldsons had been married for twenty-one years. At the time of our interviews, Jean was fifty-eight and Ned was a month away from sixty-seven. The couple had one mutual child, Penny, born a year after their marriage; and each of them had two children from their earlier relationships. Those offspring now ranged from early adulthood to early middle age. The youngest was, of course, Penny, who was twenty and attending the University of New Hampshire. Then came Jean's two children from her first marriage, a daughter, twenty-nine, and a son, thirty-three. Jean's daughter had recently given birth to a son, Jean's only grandchild thus far.

Ned's children were older. His daughter was forty-two and had three children, the oldest of whom was seven. His son, thirty-nine, was married but had no children. All four of the couple's offspring from their earlier marriages were in stable, contented relationships at that time.

Are you retired? Or if not, are you thinking about retirement; and in either case, are you thinking about meaningful, purposeful ways in which to spend your time? You, Ned, are almost sixty-seven, so is this a subject on your mind?

I like to raise the subject of retirement early in my interviews because in the majority of cases, people have usually begun giving some thought to it. Even those who are only fifty years old—which is, by the way, the official time at which the subject of gerontology begins—often have begun musing about the ways they would like their later years to take shape.

Ned told me that he had, in fact, retired three years ago. "No, wait—I retired at sixty-three, so it's actually almost four years."

"And what were you doing before that?" I asked. He'd told me that he had been a high school English teacher until they'd left Connecticut, and I wondered if he had continued teaching school in New Hampshire. But he had not. "When we went up north our thinking was that even though we had no jobs, we were a couple of smart people. So we moved into a very beautiful part of the world, and I looked for a job in my field, but there weren't any available. So I got some work with a shop where they print T-shirts. I'm an artist, among other things, and I work with silk-screen prints. So I printed thousands and thousands of silk-screen images, and sent them all over the world."

"Could you manage to make enough of a living to send your kids to college doing that?" I asked.

There was a pause, during which Ned crossed his hands in his lap like a schoolchild, and gave me a wry, downcast look. "Probably not," he said. "We probably cut our income in half by moving up to New Hampshire."

I turned to Jean and asked her how she had felt about that.

Even as I did so, I thought of her well-to-do Jewish family, for whom professional and financial success were, she had said, matters of fundamental importance.

Jean sidestepped the question by saying, "I'll tell you the truth. The fact is that I had four more years of child support. So we knew that when we moved north we could hold it together for four years. That was a kind of safety net for us; and we felt that in that time we could put something together."

She paused, then added, "I think we were both pretty committed to getting out of what was a pretty fast-track, upwardly mobile suburban life. And a simple life would not demand a whole lot of money, so I just felt . . . I didn't feel it as much of a loss as I did an adventure."

"And how about later on, when the school bills started piling up?"

There was another pause, during which Jean turned to Ned. "You tell me . . . I think we made peace with the money thing. Just by moving . . . I think we knew we were really leaving a lifestyle." He nodded.

I looked from one of them to the other. "And you decided to do that together?"

"Absolutely," Ned said. "And in terms of Penny's education, which was the only huge expenditure, we'd planned ahead and put money aside so we would be able to send her where she wanted to go. Which, interestingly, was a school which cost us forty thousand a year—and she hated it. She transferred in the middle of the year to a state school that is fifteen thousand a year."

"That's nice." I smiled. Then I turned to Jean and asked if she was retired, too. "No," she said firmly. "No." She was a clinical psychologist with a very successful practice. Before I could question her further about her career, though, Ned interrupted the conversation to say that the issues they'd had to deal with at the time of his retirement had been absolutely fascinating. "They weren't *pretty*, but they were fascinating," he stated. "Pretty" and "fascinating" were oddly lightly weighted words, I thought, to describe a time when it sounded as if there might have been some difficult issues with which they'd been confronted.

"But in answer to the question 'What do I do?' " he continued, "I am basically a creative sort of fellow, with a whole lot of ideas and projects going on in here." He pointed to the side of his head. "And I've lived a long life before coming to a time when I would be able to sit back and engage in all the creative activities that are going on inside."

Since his retirement, Ned said, he had composed a collection of choral pieces that had been published and sold on the Web to choruses across the country. He had also written a musical, which was in the stage of readings; and he was singing professionally with a couple of groups in Canada. "Some of the people I sing with are world-renowned," he said. He had collected their albums when he lived in Connecticut, but after moving to New Hampshire, he'd discovered that they were nearby neighbors.

"Somehow or other I got in with them," he said, with pride in his voice.

"So you are describing a very happy existence," I observed.

"Absolutely. It was not always thus," he hastened to add, "because at first I spent a great deal of time dealing with feelings of guilt about not having a schedule when I got up at eight o'clock in the morning. It was so different from back in the days when I knew I had to get up at eight A.M. and be out the door by eight-thirty. . . ." He let the sentence hang.

"You were a little flummoxed, then, just after you retired?" I asked.

He nodded, said that he still felt a little twitch on those mornings when Jean had to get up early for an 8 A.M. meeting with a client, while he was still yawning and stretching, about to get out of bed and into the shower. "I'll find myself saying, 'Have a nice day at the office, dear.'" His tone was rueful, and he said, "That's *not* the way I was brought up. I never saw that, as a kid. . . . But here it is." He shrugged his shoulders.

I remarked that I'd recently read Stephanie Coontz's book *Marriage, a History,* in which she states that those who are most resentful of their spouses after retirement are women who are working when their husbands are not. But that my own experience, in talking with couples, was that the retired *husbands* were lonely and the women were generally satisfied. I turned to Jean. "How do you feel about it?"

Jean took in a deep breath, and on the exhale said, "I guess I *was* a little resentful at first. That wasn't the picture I had been raised with, so it did feel a little backwards. There was also a bit of family pressure—my mother and brothers asking, 'Well, isn't he going to *do* something? Isn't he going to get a job even though he's retired?' In other words, *'Isn't he going to make some money?'"* An expression of annoyance crossed her face, and I wasn't sure whether it was meant for her family or for Ned.

"I must admit that on those days when I *did* have time to myself, I didn't like to come down and find him sitting on the couch. On those mornings when I was home and my kids were all gone I liked having the house to myself, and I thought, 'Oh, my *castle* . . .'" She hugged her arms to herself, as if to indicate a feeling of snug, contented solitude.

"So it was a shocker," I said.

She nodded. "Yes, it really was. And it overturned a lot of ideas in my mind about how I thought things should be. But there it was, I had to be the one bringing home the bread." Jean lifted her shoulders as if to say, "What could I do?" but she didn't look particularly unhappy at this moment.

I asked her if she had gotten to the other side of those feelings.

Jean smiled and said it had taken her about a year out of the three and a half years that Ned had been retired. "Now, there's a part of me that says, 'Wow, I don't want to say I support this family—not entirely—but in some ways I *do.*' And I wasn't a working mom at the beginning of my married life, so to be where I am at almost sixty, I think, 'This is *nice.*' I feel a sense of *empowerment* in doing this. I feel the separate strands between us have woven together, in terms of what we do." She went on to describe the ways in which she appreciated Ned's having dinner ready on the nights when she was working late, and the way in which he also did the dishes and cleaned the kitchen without her asking. Ned had become more of the "housekeeper person," and she enjoyed the fluidity of their gender roles. "It's a big change that has happened—not so much on the outside, but inside the two of us," she said, waving a hand that included them both.

AN INVOLUNTARY RETIREE

It is important to remember that Ned's retirement had not been one of his own desiring. It had occurred because the couple had assumed they could both find good jobs when they moved to New

Hampshire—and for a high school teacher in his late fifties, that was actually overly optimistic.

Still, it is true that Ned Donaldson was far from alone in finding himself a retiree at the age of sixty-three. In fact, the average age of retirement in this country is now between sixty and sixty-two. It is then left to the new retiree—whether eager to leave the workplace or reluctant to depart—to fashion a new and different kind of life, one that feels personally valid. Essential questions pop up: How will I spend my time? Where do I want to live? What really matters to me? Who am I, when the familiar lifelong props no longer sustain me?

I asked Ned if he had found meaningful, purposeful ways to spend his time since his retirement.

"That's the kicker," he replied. He paused, then explained in a low, somewhat troubled voice that in mid-afternoon he often asked himself what he could do so that at the end of the day he would feel that he'd accomplished something meaningful. "Because if I don't, there is this awful feeling of bouncing off the walls."

I asked him if this was the case even after he and Jean had renegotiated the terms of the relationship. Ned nodded and said this could still happen, even though they had made incredible gains after coming through a very difficult period of time. "Jean's idea of retirement and my idea of retirement just *collided,* and we had to come to an understanding—and thank God we did! But I still demand things of myself, and on the day I don't meet those demands, I don't feel very good about me."

The present problem had nothing to do with Jean, he said, for she was neither demanding nor judgmental in terms of what he did on a given day. The demands and judgments came from inside himself. "She will come home at the end of the day, and we'll be trading stories about how our day was. And I feel guilty unless I have six or eight things that I can tell her. If all I did was stack a little wood and take a nap afterward, do I tell her? I'm not sure I should. She doesn't have to hear that." He laughed a small, guilty laugh. "Anyway, I do some of my best work when I'm napping. I'm a Scorpio."

I glanced at his wife, but I couldn't read her expression.

CHANGE UPON CHANGE

I asked the Donaldsons, *"How have you been able to forgive each other's failings and betrayals (if you have)?"*

Jean smiled, as if at a question that was almost too easy to answer. "If we had to forgive each other, it never felt like a difficult thing to do." She went on to say that the connection between herself and Ned was so strong that it could easily overcome any failing or betrayal. "There's just this feeling of 'Let's work it through, and get on with it.' I don't feel that we get bogged down in that."

Ned said amiably, "Nope, we don't get bogged down." The only difficult time he could think of was that period of their lives when he was retiring and Jean was entering menopause.

"There were times when Jean's chemistry just turned her into another woman. That really depressed me. That's the reason I finally saw a therapist, the only time in my life when I've ever done so. We went together. Still, I never looked at it—at *any* of it—as being Jean's fault. I did understand what was happening. It wasn't pretty, and it wasn't fun, but we made it through, and on we go." He paused, looked at his wife searchingly, then added that he believed they had talked out everything that needed to be discussed.

Jean nodded to him, then turned to me and said there were several additional issues they'd been dealing with at the time of Ned's retirement, including the onset of her menopause and the departure of their college-bound daughter. It was the fact that these three events were happening simultaneously that had made the transition such a difficult period for both of them. "It was not a pretty picture," she said, echoing Ned's expression.

"It was tough," he said. But a brief course of couples' therapy had helped them weather the crisis. Jean said, "It was painful for me, letting go of the mother thing . . . Hard letting go of my view of myself as a youthful, middle-aged woman." For her, the advent of menopause had been freighted with ominous meanings. "It was like a trapeze bar heading straight toward me—and so I had to reach out and grab for it, and that meant letting go and leaving what I had behind me, and that was very scary, very hard work."

"So you felt like you were letting go of a whole way of life?" I asked her.

She nodded. "And everything in me was resisting! I was thinking, 'Oh my God, they tell me it's going to be good, but I don't really believe it. I just want to leave things as they are, I *like* my life the way it is!' "

"It was brutal," Ned said, in a downcast tone of voice.

Jean met and held his gaze. "I think we pulled out of a really knotty place," she said, speaking to him, not to me. Then, turning her attention to me, she reiterated that they'd been dealing with an avalanche of money issues, separation issues and her own physiological changes at the same time. But it was behind them, she added—and this had been especially true over the past six to nine months, when she had experienced an ever-increasing sense of peacefulness.

I looked from one to the other. "So you two really made a decision for the simple life, right?"

"Yes, absolutely," Jean said, and Ned said, "Absolutely," in almost the same breath.

I asked them how they felt about that decision.

Ned said without hesitation that he'd felt blessed from the day they decided. "I don't even know how I got so lucky as to know this was an option!" he added enthusiastically.

Jean said, with equal enthusiasm, that she would never, ever, do it any other way. "I only wish I had done it sooner. *A simple life*. A simple, *meaningful* life. Meaningful work, but not where money becomes the motivation." She went on to say that she, too, felt blessed. "Blessed to find a man who has the depth of feeling and the depth of love for me and the kindness that Ned has. I love that in him, and I love that he lives and expresses himself quite comfortably in those ways," she declared softly.

This prompted me to turn to Ned and ask, "If you were going to give a title to a movie or a book about this time of your life, what do you think it would be?"

Ned laughed. "Oh, I don't know. Probably *Set Free*." He blushed slightly.

"*Set Free*," I repeated. "You mean you're who you are, and not in any kind of prison of your own or anyone else's making?"

"Absolutely. I'm more of who I am, and *what* I am, with no bounds or bonds, than ever before in my life," he said.

I turned to Jean questioningly, who thought for a moment and said, "That's a hard one. For me, it's like throwing open doors and welcoming . . . I don't know. *Life in Bloom*, or something like that, would be my title."

"You ought to see her garden," Ned said.

THE WAY IT WAS

A question I usually reserve for the concluding section of my interviews with couples over fifty is, *What do you think are the major sexual issues that emerge at this time of life?*

Actually, Jean Donaldson herself had raised the topic of sex much earlier. She had interrupted a conversation in which we were discussing the general mood-tone of this time of their lives. I'd asked the Donaldsons to describe it—"happy," "sad," "mixed," whatever.

Ned had responded without hesitation, "I think, generally happy. I would say that we love getting up in the morning, and we love going to bed at night. We have these huge sliding glass doors that look out on a vista you simply wouldn't believe! And it's just . . . seeing the sun come up, the moon or the stars. Just looking around when we walk out the front door! When we drive home, and into our little parking area, we look around, every time, and we say, 'Wow!' . . . Don't we?" He turned to Jean.

She nodded at him, smiling, but then said to me, "You know, I think I have to tell you something. Because the picture that's emerging here is so flawless and so perfect, and I really want to make sure . . . I think that sexually things are very different."

"We'll get to that eventually," I had assured her.

"Okay, good," she said. "Because I don't want to be evasive or hold back."

"It's an energy thing," Ned said, comfortably.

I wasn't sure what he meant, but at that particular point in the interview I decided to let the comment pass by without question.

Now there was a silence, which I broke by saying to Jean, "You wanted to get to the issue of sex?" She shook her head in the negative, then said she hadn't really *wanted* to but felt she had to be honest. She knew that the purpose of my study was to get information out to my readers, and that the accuracy of the picture I presented would be as important to them as it would be to her.

There was another silence, which ended when Jean murmured something about not knowing how far back to go. Then she cleared her throat and said, "Basically I'm not a sexually extravagant person. I've had two sexual partners, my first husband and my second husband. Ned said that for him it was like marrying a virgin! In every sense sex for me is an intimate experience—the union of two souls—but I don't necessarily have this extravagant, flamboyant aspect. It might be nice, you know, but it's not what I'm doing in this lifetime."

I heard her to be saying that lusty sex had never been at the top of the list of her priorities. But she went on to say that the sexual intimacy they'd shared before her menopause had always been very important to the relationship because it made them both feel so close. "We would talk about it for days afterward. . . . It was just really . . . delicious. It was wonderful."

At that time, she had felt so securely *in her body;* but the last time they'd had sex, it had hurt; it didn't feel right; nothing arousing had been happening. "I felt as if my whole sexual apparatus was foreign to me. It's not so much to do with physical energy, but a whole feeling that my body is different. It's not the body I've known throughout my life."

"You mean, postmenopausally?" I asked.

"Yup," Jean replied.

SEX AND AGING

Jean Donaldson's belief that her "sexual apparatus" had undergone changes during the menopausal years was surely grounded in reality. Both women *and* men experience differences in their sexuality with the passage of time—changes due to subtle, internal developments that have been quietly occurring as they move onward in their adult lives. Although these slow, organically based shifts in sexual functioning are a normal part of growing older, both males and females often lack basic information about what is happening within their bodies, and what sorts of changes are to be expected. In such instances, a natural aspect of the process of aging can readily be construed as a sexual problem that is unique to a particular individual.

Here are some of the things that happen as a woman ages: her vagina is typically slower to lubricate during foreplay, and therefore an extended period of nongenital lovemaking (kissing, stroking) should be part of the agenda. The female's delayed responsiveness is, by the way, physiologically similar to the aging male's longer time to achieve erection. In both cases—lubrication and erection—the desired effects are eventually produced by congestion of the blood vessels in the vaginal or penile walls; but it is easy to see why a person who doesn't understand this normal increase in timing might interpret it as lack of interest or a feared rejection by the sexual partner.

Also, as women age, their vaginal tissues begin to thin and they may become easily irritated, especially if sufficient lubrication isn't present, which in turn can lead to painful intercourse (aka dyspareunia). If sex is being experienced as unpleasant or downright harmful, it doesn't take a great leap of the imagination to understand why Jean was not feeling that the "right," arousing things were happening.

Painful sex can cause a person's body musculature to stiffen; Jean might have begun fearing a hurtful experience more than she was anticipating a joyful union with Ned.

I asked her if she thought her feelings of being in a less friendly, less recognizable body might have something to do with the drying vaginal tissues that accompany aging.

Jean nodded, and added that she had read a book and taken some kind of "sexual inventory" that made her realize that she probably had a very low libido—low testosterone and probably low estrogen—and that these hormone deficits were probably showing up in her current state of disinterest. "So, not to be sexually arousable—to just not *feel* it, to not *want* it. I mean I just don't have that thing perking in me!"

I asked her how long this feeling of "rather not" had been going on.

Jean looked at Ned as if expecting him to reply, but he shrugged. "Just recently, it got a little better . . . but it started about two years ago," she said. I thought about the fact that this was the period of their lives when Ned retired and Jean was mourning the loss of her self-concept as a youthful, actively mothering, middle-aged woman.

"But it's still nothing like the way it was . . . ?" Jean shook her head no. I hesitated, then asked, "Do you feel as if you've never been sexually awakened? Is that what I hear you saying?"

Jean shook her head again, said, "No, no . . . I mean, I felt . . . I feel . . ." She halted and left her thought unfinished.

After a pause, I asked quietly, "Do you feel like you've gone into a bit of a shutdown?"

She nodded her agreement and said, "I feel like the shutdown happened when I went into menopause. I felt, before that time, that I'd been truly awakened in my relationship with Ned. But what I meant to say was this: it wasn't that sex per se was ever such a pervasive part of my life; it was that, between us, it was a very intimate, special thing. Then menopause came, and what used to work wasn't really working. I was probably a bit depressed during that period, and my feeling was just 'Leave me alone.' Then, when I started to come out of it, I didn't want to use hormone therapy. So I read a lot of books on the subject, and I got the herbal remedies that I thought would enhance . . ." Again, she stopped short of completing her sentence.

"That would help you . . . ?"

"Yes, and maybe they did help; or maybe things just leveled out on their own. Maybe my own system took over what my ovaries weren't doing. It *is* better now. I do have an orgasm. I can get to that place without . . . you know . . . too much difficulty. But I don't have that eagerness, that 'Let's do it!' feeling, not at all."

I asked her if she had feelings of anxiety when the idea of having sex was in the air. Jean shook her head and said she felt more anxious about the idea *not* coming up. She worried about why she didn't feel it, so much so that sometimes she would say, "Let's just go do it, and give it a shot."

I glanced at Ned to see how he was responding to his wife speaking of her misgivings and lack of enthusiasm. He was sitting in an almost military posture, upright on the sofa, his expression conveying nothing.

Jean said that she *did* want to go on having sex, no matter what, because she was afraid that "if you don't use it, you lose it." "I don't want to get all dry and shriveled up. Still, I wonder how much of this is cultural pressure. I mean, we were watching one of the morning news shows—maybe *Good Morning America*—and they were saying that people our age have sex on average one and a half times a week. And we looked at each other in horror—"

"Oh, my God!" Ned said, and they both laughed. I laughed, too, said I wondered what the "half" referred to. Then I added that the only statistics I'd encountered thus far suggested that people their age had sex an average of every two weeks.

"We're still not making it. We try to shoot for once a month." Ned raised his shoulders briefly, as if to say, "What can you do?"

I asked Jean if she typically experienced pain because of vaginal dryness. She said that they had begun using lubrication. "Initially I didn't like the idea, but I use it now; and if I just hang in there, it gets better." Her basic lack of libidinous inclination was so clearly apparent in her expression and her tone of voice.

"So the question on your mind is, 'Why don't I feel differently?' " I inquired.

Jean's gaze was fixed on me, and I met her eyes directly. She didn't answer, just nodded her agreement. There was a long, tension-filled silence.

I turned to her husband. "What's your take on this, Ned?"

I was taken aback, if not to say dumbfounded, when he responded with a light shrug of his shoulders and said in an even voice, "To be honest, I believe I got there before Jean did. . . . I remember the days when I realized my desires were fading away." At that moment I flashed on his saying how much he had treasured their close, platonic friendship in its earliest days, a time when he wasn't being called upon to "perform" sexually. I thought, too, about the ways in which one partner's "fading desires" can affect the other partner, whose own levels of desire adapt and adjust to those of the cherished mate.

MALE SEXUAL AGING

It is the belief of Dr. Robert N. Butler, coauthor of the excellent *Sex After Sixty*, that even males in their thirties begin feeling secret apprehensions about changes in their sexuality. They start noticing and comparing their sexual performance with the way it was when they were adolescents or in young adulthood. Such concerns begin to multiply as men pass through the decades of the forties, the fifties and, ultimately, the sixties; by then, noticeable and definite sexual changes are ordinarily present.

Such changes in the aging male's sexuality are normal and, generally speaking, amenable to clear-eyed understanding and management. In these older years, a man is somewhat slower to reach an erection and—especially early in the sexual encounter—his erection will often be less sturdy than it was earlier in his life.

This can sometimes lead to misunderstandings between the members of the couple. For if both partners do not understand this slowness to reach erection as a normal part of sexual aging, the female partner is liable to feel rejected—especially considering that we live in a youth-intoxicated society, one in which an older woman may assume that his changed sexuality is due to the fact that her sexual attractiveness is fading.

Butler and coauthor Myra Lewis write: "The difference [in timing to reach erection] is a matter of minutes after sexual stimulation rather than a few seconds. The erection may not be as large, straight, and hard as in previous years. Once the man is fully excited, however, the erection will usually be sturdy and reliable if this was the pattern in earlier life."

The *crucial* thing to remember is that manual (or oral) stimulation of the male's organ by his partner is usually all that is necessary in order to promote and maintain his state of sexual arousal. In those instances where the female is unwilling to do this, the male may stimulate his own penis; but it is obviously more mutual and loving if this is an enterprise that involves both of them. In any event, it is *vital* to realize that manual or oral stimulation of the older male's penis may be viewed as the starter motor that will promote erotic arousal and set the sexual encounter in motion.

Another change that an aging male may notice is that, over time, the lubrication that used to appear just before ejaculation has decreased or disappeared entirely. This has little effect on his sexual performance. According to Butler and Lewis, older males *also* experience a reduction in the volume of seminal fluid: younger men produce three to five milliliters (about a teaspoon) every twenty-four hours, while men over fifty produce two to three milliliters. This in turn reduces the intensity of the pressure to ejaculate.

This little-known but intriguing fact of nature can lead to one of the glorious boons of lovemaking in the older years. The male is under far less internal, physiologically based pressure to reach orgasm, and is therefore more able to control and delay his ejaculation. As expert Butler explains, "The older man can make love longer. This in turn extends his own enjoyment and enhances the possibility of orgasm/pleasure for his partner."

Speaking in broad, general terms, it is known that sexual intercourse does decrease in frequency over the course of a long-term relationship. However, as authors Marilyn Yalom and Laura Carstensen point out in *Inside the American Couple*, a couple's sex life usually doesn't cease completely unless it's due to the illness of one of the mates. And although there are *some* older couples who stop all sexual

contact, write Yalom and Carstensen, "many other older people report
that sexual activity improves with age. In part *because* intercourse and
orgasm are less central, lovemaking can grow more relaxed and emotionally intimate." While there are changes in sexual functioning over
the course of a marriage, maintain the authors, " 'asexual' does not
well characterize them."

A PLACE THAT IS FAR MORE NOURISHING

What about couples who, like the Donaldsons, feel that perhaps they
"ought" to have more sex, but don't really feel the internal push to do
so? Some older couples feel content to engage in sexual activities far
less often or to wind down their erotic lives completely. This is a problem *only* if one member of the couple is unhappy with the situation,
and sex has become a source of conflict in the relationship.

Was their low sex drive a problem for Jean and Ned Donaldson, or
was it simply Jean's problem? Earlier on, she had said that she'd had
two erotic partners in her lifetime—her two husbands—and that she
was not an "extravagantly, flamboyantly" sexual woman. Although
she was clearly an affectionate and loving person, she gave me the
impression that she'd never been hugely interested in the sexual act
per se. Individual, biologically based differences and early social
messages about sex do play a role in shaping an individual's eventual
sexual profile, and not every female grows up to be a sex bomb. Jean
had certainly indicated that she herself wasn't one, at least "not in this
lifetime."

Ned's sexual history had been totally different. "Jean describes having had two partners," he said. "But way back then I lived an entirely
different kind of life, one that was very wild and very sexual." He
spoke in a low voice.

"This was between marriages?" I asked.

He nodded, said that to be honest, it went on *during* his first marriage, too. "That was just one of the saddest and the sickest relationships there ever was, and a great deal of it was caused by my wife, who was doing who knows what and with whom. I often had my closest friends come up to me and tell me you'd better keep an eye on her, she's trying to seduce me. This would be going on at a party." He looked disgusted and contemptuous, an expression I'd not seen on his face throughout the interview. He shrugged his shoulders as if shrugging off an offensive memory. "So . . . I had many relationships, sexual relationships, during that time." He didn't seem particularly nostalgic or even pleased by the recollection.

I asked Ned how old he was when he began to feel his desires start to fade. He believed he had been around sixty, and that it worried him a lot at the time. His major concern had been that the next time that Jean wanted to have sex—"or the next time that we really *should* have sex"—he might be nowhere near in the mood for it. "It felt so strange to me because here we were in a situation where it's a wonderful night, and we're in bed lying close to each other . . . and by God, if I was ten years younger I'd have been jumping all over the place! But the feeling wasn't there." He fell silent, and his gaze dropped and became fixed on the hands folded in his lap.

After a long pause, I asked him if he thought he'd been experiencing some performance anxiety. At once, Ned raised his eyes and said, "Absolutely! I still do. Yes, that's what's been going on with me."

I looked from one member of the couple to the other, wondering which was the chicken and which was the egg in this cycle of declining libido. It would have been easy to pathologize what was going on here: Jean's menopause—her loss of reproductive capacity and view of herself as a "youthful, actively mothering, middle-aged woman"—

may have signaled to her the symbolic ending of her life as a sexual female. Or alternatively, Ned's retirement, and the couple's subsequent dependence on Jean's income, could have led to a situation in which he felt de-masculinized—and therefore "unable to get it up."

But the powerful devotion and regard these partners shared was a palpable presence in the room. It was manifest in their body language—the ways they inclined toward each other—and in the glances they exchanged, which were full of respect and affection. It was manifest in the manner in which they spoke, and in which they listened to what the other person had to say. The Donaldsons were not an unhappy couple.

I said, choosing my words carefully, "It sounds as if you two have a tremendously loving relationship, and yet there's an undercurrent of worry about why things are happening as they are." Both of them nodded. I asked if they'd thought about using one of the erection-enhancing drugs such as Viagra. I laughed, said, "It is, you know, one of the best-selling drugs in America!"

"Yes, I know it is," Ned responded evenly.

I went on to say that this would be a way of reducing his anxiety about performance, and a pretty rational one, at that. It might very well have an effect on Jean's sense of "shutdown," too: "I think a woman often feels rejected and anxious when the sexual experience doesn't work out," I added, then stopped in mid-paragraph. Jean's expression had hardened.

"*I* don't feel rejected and anxious in that situation," she said. "I feel rejected when Ned doesn't say, 'Let's cuddle up.' I feel more rejected at his not wanting to get close. You know, we've talked about this, and it's my feeling that there is something *artificial* about drugs like Viagra. And I don't want him taking anything that could be harmful. I'm just against it."

I asked her if she felt that the present impasse was, in its own way, harmful.

"No, I don't," Jean responded firmly.

I turned to her husband. "How do you feel about it, Ned?" I inquired.

He was silent for a brief space of time. Then he said, speaking slowly and thoughtfully, "What's been running through my mind as I heard this conversation going on is the thought that . . . that if sex is intercourse and intercourse only, then this is something that needs further discussion. But if sex is physically loving one another—if it's hopping into bed and curling up tightly next to each other, so close that you are almost melted into one body . . . if it's waking up in the morning and not allowing your partner to get out of bed before kissing her delicious self good morning . . . then we have *lots* of sex." He was blushing. He turned to his wife and fixed her with that long, fixed, unblinking gaze that is rightly known as "eye love."

We were quiet. Eventually, Jean turned to me. "I don't know that 'undercurrent of worry' is the phrase I would use. To me, it's a loss. A loss of youth. A loss of those days when we would just look at each other and couldn't *wait* to hop into bed! But guess what? I'm not thirty-five years old anymore! And there's a part of me that feels that the relationship has moved into a place that's far more nourishing and satisfying than what sex accomplishes. Because it's very true, as Ned was just saying, that the physical contact that we have on a daily basis—and this *connection* that we feel—" Here she halted, reached both arms toward her husband in a gesture that signified her pulling him toward her.

Then she dropped her hands into her lap, said again that she didn't feel it was worth it to her for Ned to take Viagra. "No, that just doesn't feel *right* to me. I think we are still playful enough with each other,

and open enough with each other, to experiment and say, 'Hey, sometimes it works and sometimes it doesn't; and we don't leave in a worse
place because of that. . . . I don't feel any less connected to him."

It was at that moment that I realized that neither Jean nor her husband was actually hungry for change. On the contrary, the Donaldsons
were at peace, and in a place that was deeply satisfying to both
of them.

Chapter Six

JACKIE AND STEVE WINSTON (1)

TRANSITIONING:

A FOOT IN EACH WORLD

The Winstons' decision to sell their large home in the upscale
Boston suburb of Belmont, Massachusetts, and move to an
attractive colony of condominiums designed for older-adult
living was prompted by a variety of concerns. One of them was
Jackie Winston's growing sense of isolation. The house in Belmont felt
so big and too empty now that the children were grown and had
moved on to start family lives of their own. Jackie, at age sixty-two,
was a much-admired architect, and had recently stepped down as
chairman of her local chapter of the American Architectural Association. At present, she was no longer working at the furious pace she
had earlier, but she was still putting in several long, hard days a week
at her firm.

Jackie truly enjoyed her successful, personally rewarding career,
but she was dealing with several vexing health issues at this time. As
she told me in a lowered, confiding tone of voice, these were things
she didn't speak about with most people. One had to do with her hear-

ing, which had become compromised in her forties, and was now seriously affected. Jackie wore hearing aids in both ears, but she would often fail to hear a comment from across a table—and she had the notion ("I know it's paranoid") that when that happened, people thought she was dull-witted or dumb.

The second health problem she was dealing with was DCIS—ductal carcinoma in situ. This is breast cancer in its very earliest stage.

"You don't have a lumpectomy. You don't have chemo, high radiation," Jackie explained, with a shrug of her slender shoulders, as if to say this was nothing particularly important. Then she laughed. "You can tell that I minimize—I'm very good at minimizing. I mean I do everything I'm supposed to do, get checked out by all the doctors that I need to see. But I'm pretty good at compartmentalizing. I mean, sometimes I have to remind myself, oh yes, I had that . . ." She didn't complete her sentence by uttering the world "cancer" aloud.

Nevertheless, the word hung in the air. I gazed at her, telegraphing my sympathy in a prolonged, understanding look. "How was it discovered?" I asked at last. A scared expression flitted across Jackie's face, and she ran a quick hand through her tightly curly blond hair. "Mammography," she answered briefly. Then she reiterated that fortunately her condition was not very serious, and she had "sort of tucked it away."

Jackie's mammography had revealed several calcifications in one of her breasts, and when the calcifications had been removed, they were found to contain malignant cells. But there had been no invasion of the ductal wall, she said, "so it's not so much a problem as it is the *precursor* of a possible problem." Again she shrugged her shoulders, as if to dismiss the issue's importance. The cancer threat had been discovered several years before, when Jackie had just turned fifty-nine. But it was neither of these health concerns—nor her sense of isolation in a large house that still held echoes of a busy family life—that had ultimately motivated the Winstons to move into their countrified older-adults' village. Rather, it was an alarming experience—something that had happened to her husband, Steve, about a year and a half earlier.

I turned to Steven (Steve) Winston, who is an M.D. with a specialty in hematology. We were meeting in his large, comfortable office in a medical building not far from one of the Harvard-connected hospitals. The couple sat on a short upholstered love seat, and Steve's arm was stretched across the sofa's back and his wife's shoulders. I was sitting on one of two comfortable chairs directly opposite them.

"What *was* this alarming experience?" I asked Steve directly. At the same time I was thinking about how much this friendly-looking man resembled a beloved uncle of my husband's, who had also been a physician and who'd had the same full head of softly waving silvery hair.

Before responding, Steve hesitated for several moments. He placed a hand on each of his knees, leaned forward and stared at the back of his hands for a while. Finally, he raised his head and fixed his gaze on mine. His eyes were large and gray-green in color. He sighed, then said that it had happened when he was driving down from Boston to see his son and daughter-in-law, who live in Stamford, Connecticut. Jackie wasn't with him; she was visiting her elderly father in Florida.

"From what I can gather, I pulled into the last rest stop on the Mass. Turnpike, and I guess I was just sitting there, feeling confused. Why was I here? Because this *wasn't* the stop where Jackie and I usually pull off. We go to a little place which is just outside Hartford, where we gas up and use the facilities and maybe buy some doughnuts and coffee."

Steve shrugged his shoulders briefly, looking bewildered at this moment.

It was then, he went on, that his cell phone began to ring. It was his son Paul calling—a routine call to check on his dad's whereabouts and when he was expecting to arrive. These were questions that Steve Winston had found himself unable to answer.

"I'm not really sure *where* I am," he'd told his son, in a baffled tone of voice, "but I'm just sitting here, parked at a gas station, and I'm waiting for Mom to come out of the bathroom."

"But Paul said, 'Dad, Dad . . . Mom *can't* be coming out of the bathroom—she's in Florida!' "

Steve paused in his telling of the story.

"Frightening," I said, into the momentary silence.

"Exactly." He nodded, then said that he'd been very, very frightened at the time. "At least, so I was told afterward. Much of my memory of this whole incident is foggy, in bits and pieces. I don't even remember driving down the Pike as far as I did."

Steve's son, alarmed, told him to hit the OnStar button in his car. This is a global positioning device that has a number of features, one of which is to summon help, if needed. Paul also told his father to take his keys and cell phone, then get out of the car and go find somebody—anybody—who might be willing to help him. "So I got out and went up to this stranger, a lady, who later told me that I was completely petrified. I don't remember this part. I don't remember a thing."

Steve had handed his car keys and cell phone to this kind stranger, who returned to the car with him at once. There, she held a hurried conversation with his son. "So, after that, to make a long story short . . ." He paused, took a deep breath, his expression uncertain.

I cocked my head to one side, as if to say, "Go on."

But after a short silence, Jackie chimed in. "The woman called an ambulance," she said.

"They all thought he'd had a stroke."

"It sure sounds like one," I said, speculatively.

"*Doesn't* it?" Steve asked, then shook his head to indicate that it hadn't been one. His son had quickly alerted Jackie's older brother, who is a lawyer in Stamford. He, in turn, had immediately left his office and picked up his nephew Paul. "The pair of them started driving north without even knowing what hospital I was being taken to. They located me in the hospital I was rushed to—that was in Hartford—and I was there for three days. I've been told that every single test known to mankind was given to me. I mean *everything!*" Steve said.

The attending physicians had found no sign of a stroke, no sign of any cerebral event whatsoever. "There was nothing, but *nothing*—just a clear brain here—the brain, they told me, of a much younger man. But my memory of that whole period is pretty much nil. I'm not sure, but I'd say I lost about five or six days in all. I don't remember being in the hospital; I don't remember going home, even though I was well enough to go home."

He shrugged again. "I took two weeks off from work, and then I went back to the office and that's it."

"He was fine, everything was okay," Jackie said quickly, running her hand through her curly hair again—a nervous habit of hers, I realized.

TRANSIENT GLOBAL AMNESIA

Steve Winston had experienced an episode of a relatively unknown complaint called transient global amnesia (TGA). This condition is unrelated to any neurologic signs and has no epileptic features. People who suffer an episode of TGA become disoriented and confused, Steve told me, but, unlike stroke victims, they know their own names and remain aware of their identities.

Most attacks of TGA last one to eight hours, rarely longer than a day. Therefore, Steve's four- to five-day period of disorientation and memory loss was on the outer edge of the typical curve. I asked him if he knew the chances of it ever happening again.

He said there was, roughly speaking, a 25 percent chance of a recurrence, and I asked him where he'd gotten that figure.

"Neurologists, who told me about it," he said. "Driving is the primary precipitating factor. That is, driving alone."

"Why is that?" I asked, and he said that driving is a situation in which it is easy to zone out. Another precipitating factor is swimming in cold water, he added, and a third is sex.

"Sex is another one," echoed Jackie.

"Yep, those are the big three," Steve said.

"Those are the big three." Jackie repeated his words once again.

Later on, however, I read in the literature on TGA that physical or emotional stress can be a causative factor as well. To my surprise, I also found that this ailment is not as rare as I supposed: roughly speaking, some twenty-three thousand people who are age fifty and over suffer an episode of transient global amnesia each year. Generally speaking, these individuals are completely healthy otherwise.

Nevertheless, this was a life-changing event for the Winstons—

both in the large sense of deciding to move into an older adults–
oriented community and in a number of small, daily ways as well.
Steve showed me the large identification tag he always wore, like an
amulet, around his neck. "This is in case I'm found somewhere and I'm
confused and feeling lost and scared. It explains what my condition is,
and who I am, and who is the person to call.

"I also carry a letter in my wallet, and when I'm driving alone I put
it on the front seat. It says that if I am found in a confused state to
please call Jackie, and it gives her phone number."

"Which is great, it makes me feel a lot better," Jackie said. "As you
can imagine, I kept him on a pretty short leash for a while. I was so
worried and scared."

Many months—more than a year and a half—had now passed
since that incident, and nothing further had occurred. I wondered
how much it bothered the Winstons at present. "How much do you
think about it?" I asked them, my tone of voice tentative.

The couple exchanged a long, questioning look, as if each one was
waiting for the other to respond. Then Steve said slowly, "I do think
about it. I feel . . . when I drive down to Stamford, or to New York, I
feel . . ." He left the sentence unfinished.

"I believe you *do* think about it," Jackie said to Steve. "You tend to
overlook some of the normal forgetting of getting older, and you get
nervous. I'll ask you if you remember such and such, and if you've forgotten, I can see the panicked look on your face."

Steve's cheeks flushed slightly, and he smiled somewhat shamefacedly. "It's true. If I'm on my way to work and I'm having trouble
remembering something, I immediately pull this identification out."
He had put the tag out of sight underneath his blue shirt, but now he
displayed it to me once again. "So of course it's always on my mind. I

usually put it on over my coat, so someone doesn't have to start undressing me to find out who I am and what to do. Obviously, it's always something I'm thinking about. Especially when I drive to work in the morning."

The incident had affected him in a number of other ways, his wife said thoughtfully. Shortly after that episode, Steve decided to make a change in his work life. He sold his share of his medical practice to his younger colleagues, and now he took a full day and a couple of afternoons off every week. Jackie thought it had also impacted *both* of them in still different, subtler ways that would be very hard to explain. "It was like a little gong or buzzer sounding, for both of us," she said earnestly. "It was a buzzer saying, 'Yes, it's time to check this out. You're at a different place in your life.'"

A SHIFTING SENSE OF TIME

Many theorists of middle age and aging have noted that somewhere in the fifty-plus years, most men and women experience an inner shift in their sense of time's directionality. They are no longer thinking of their age in backward-looking terms, in the sense of time-since-birth; they are now reckoning forward in terms of the years they may have left to live. This happens because they have begun confronting— as never before—the fact that their sojourn on earth is limited and will eventually come to a close.

Jackie Winston, at age sixty-two, described this subjective shift as a "buzzer," a dispatch from the universe that they were now moving into a new stage of their existence. In their case, this period of their lives was likely to be a long one. In the early twenty-first century, individuals who reach their mid-sixties in reasonably good (not perfect) health can expect to live another eighteen to twenty years, or longer. So the Winstons could look forward to many years of relatively active and engaged living.

True, the couple had recently cut back their work hours and moved into an adult community in response to their medical concerns. However, this was not because either of them was infirm or disabled; it was because they wanted to preserve their current state of health and extend their years of well-being as long as possible. The Winstons had arrived at a time of their lives that social scientists call the "third age"; that is, the extended years of "young-old" living between fifty and seventy-five that have become incorporated into the ordinary life span during the course of this past century.

In my own view, as mentioned earlier, this phase of later adulthood is a *mirror* of the adolescent period, because in both cases so many fundamental life changes are suddenly demanded. Adolescents and young adults are in the process of forming a work identity; individuals in late adulthood are in the process of leaving a long-habituated work identity behind them. Adolescents and young adults are deciding where to live, and with whom; older adults are often leaving behind emptying family homes and moving to age-graded communities where they become more and more involved (like teenagers) with their age-group peers.

One difference, as we saw in Laura Carstensen's research, is that adolescents and young adults often seek friendships with people who may one day be helpful to them in their career endeavors. Older adults are far less interested in the potential usefulness of interesting new acquaintances; they are far more engaged in forging real emotional connections with important people in their close circle of friends and relations.

It is, incidentally, worth noting that adolescents and young adults often seek somewhat older mentor figures as stand-ins for the parents who were their former guides through earlier times. Older adults, for their own part, seem to enjoy filling this nurturing role. Indeed, men and women in later adulthood often continue to mentor younger colleagues throughout the "third age" of their own lives.

This quasi-parenting usually doesn't happen in the retired adult's former work setting, but older people with wisdom and know-how often find manifold ways to pass their knowledge along to these younger members of the workforce who are eager to receive it. An example of this phenomenon is an organization called SCORE (Service Corps of Retired Executives), which is dedicated to linking up new businesses and the many older, highly qualified retirees who are glad to donate their confidential, well-seasoned skills and expertise.

THIS RECENT INNOVATION CALLED RETIREMENT

The word "retirement" derives from the French word *retirer,* which means "to withdraw." Needless to say, in current parlance this connotes a withdrawal from the workforce. Retirement—a period of socially condoned leisure and freedom from labor in later adulthood—is now an ingrained feature of the life-course, but it wasn't always so. At one time, this "life stage" didn't even exist.

In the early 1900s a person's average life expectancy was roughly age fifty, and in general, most workers remained on the job until they were too sick to continue. It was the passage of the Social Security Act in 1935 that introduced a new, federally supported phase of living called "retirement" as the anticipated coda of the life span. An individual became eligible for this pension at the age of sixty-five.

Still, in the mid-1930s, a working man's average longevity had risen to only 59.7 years, so there were not many people who lived long enough to enjoy this new period of socially approved, responsibility-free living. When someone did survive long enough to leave the workplace at the prescribed age of sixty-five, it was tacitly understood that he was nearing the end of his life. The typical length of time a person spent as a retiree was no more than three years, or 7 percent of his adult existence.

For this reason, the advent of liberty from one's labors, and a welcome absence of responsibility, had an equivocal quality: it marked both the arrival of freedom and a simultaneous movement into the antechamber of mortality.

However, as the decades of the twentieth century rolled by and our life span continued to lengthen, the word "retirement" began to lose many of its negative connotations. The "afternoon of life," as Carl Jung called the later adult years, had become not only an elongated period of time; it was also receiving financial support from additional sources. In the middle 1950s, for example, the increasingly powerful unions began bargaining for higher pensions for workers, most of which were along the lines of "defined-benefits" plans.

These kinds of pensions guarantee the retiree a fixed monthly income. Defined-benefits pensions are usually funded *entirely* by employers and automatically cover all qualified employees. This generous type of retirement plan made sense in the post–World War II period, when America was extremely wealthy and the pool of retirees was small.

From the employer's point of view, this pension plan served as a means of guaranteeing the employee's loyalty and commitment to the company, for the monthly sum conferred at retirement typically reflected the number of years the employee had been with the firm and also the status and salary he or she had attained. Also, these ample pensions provided for the orderly departure of older adults from the workplace, at the mandatory age of sixty-five, which was an effective means of freeing up their jobs for the younger men who had returned from overseas.

As the years passed, however, the defined-benefits pension plans proved to be increasingly impractical, for as one wave of retirees succeeded another, it brought many companies under mounting economic pressure. Employers were completely responsible for funding these pensions, and in many instances, company managers began to raid the monies earmarked as pension funds and use them for completely different purposes. The manifold problems plaguing these retirement arrangements led to a situation in which hundreds of companies (including behemoths such as General Motors, Ford, IBM and Boeing) eventually held pension plans that were seriously underfunded. Even the government agency set up to ensure these defined-benefits plans (the Participant Benefits Guarantor Corporation, or PBGC) found itself in difficulties, for it, too, became underfunded eventually. As financial journalist Laura Bruce has written: "With so many companies drowning and their pensions being taken over by the PBGC, the rescuer is now in need of a life preserver."

For the above reasons, defined-benefits plans have fallen out of favor and a completely different kind of pension instrument—the so-called defined-contributions plan—has emerged and become the arrangement of choice. This type of pension plan is quite different from the defined-benefits kind, for the employee is *not* promised a fixed amount of money upon retirement. Instead, he or she contributes a certain amount of money from his monthly paycheck (which is typically tax-deductible), and the employer puts in an equal or somewhat different sum on a regular basis. The total sum of these joint employee/employer contributions, as it accumulates in the retirement fund, is *under the control of the employee.*

The employee may then be cautious and invest all of the money in bonds. Or he or she can be adventurous and invest in the stock market, or create a portfolio that is a combination of stocks and bonds. Sometimes the employee can invest most of the pension fund in a particular stock; and here it needs to be said that one of the big problems that retirees have had is that of naively investing all or most of their pension funds in their own company's stock.

This typically happens at the employer's urging, and it can cause serious problems. First of all, the worker's investments are then *not* sensibly diversified in a variety of stocks and perhaps some bonds as well; and second, the worth of the retiree's pension rises and falls with the company's fortunes. This was what happened in the Enron situation, where employees who were in a defined-contributions arrangement listened to the assurances of their unscrupulous bosses and invested their pension funds in the giant firm's stock. They were left without any retirement assets after the company's collapse.

But that situation was an aberration; generally speaking, these defined-contributions retirement arrangements (which have familiar names such as IRA and Keogh plans) prove very satisfactory. One of their virtues is that if a person changes jobs, he can bring his accumulated retirement benefits to the new place of employment. Also, a *major* virtue of these plans is that as the value of the employee's investments appreciates, he or she does not have to pay taxes on the additional wealth until he chooses to withdraw the funds from the plan. This contributes to the steady growth of the pension because that

untaxed money can then be reinvested and earn monies that will fos-
ter further growth of the employee's nest egg. There *is* a downside,
however, because the retiree does have to pay income taxes when the
funds are eventually withdrawn. This is a serious drawback because
income taxes are higher than capital gains taxes. So in this instance,
the investor is making a calculated trade-off, but the choices he makes
are his own.

In brief, the great distinction between the older, traditional
defined-benefits pension plans and the currently preferred defined-
contributions plans is this: in the first instance, the employer provides
and *controls* the pension funds; in the second instance, it is the
employee who takes charge of his own pension fund and makes his
own retirement decisions. This provides the retiree with a greater mar-
gin of personal decision-making and long-run safety.

The home mortgage interest deduction is, along with Social
Security and the varying types of pension plans, also something wor-
thy of notice here. For as the well-known sociologist David Ekerdt told
me, in the course of a conversation, "This, too, was a retirement
device. Nobody thinks of it that way, but the fact is that it *did* help
people to build wealth over the years." It built wealth by effectively
lowering the home owner's taxes; the mortgage holder's taxable
income per year was decreased by the amount of his yearly interest
payments. Moreover, very importantly, during the second half of the
twentieth century the value of housing in this country appreciated
dramatically. A couple's home is now often the primary asset owned
by the partners upon retirement.

Yet another boon to prospective retirees was the introduction of
Medicare in 1965. This plan made it possible for people to conceive
of retirement without the dread of leaving their health insurance

behind. And shortly after Medicare was passed into federal law, a steady increase in Social Security benefits got under way: between 1968 and 1971 retirees' stipends rose by 43 percent while the cost of living rose only 27 percent. Then, in 1972, Social Security benefits were upped by another whopping 20 percent. By this time, the idea of retiring in advance of any serious disability had become a widespread expectation—a built-in, standard feature of the life span rather than the dubious, even unthinkable idea it had been a hundred years earlier.

To be sure, a certain minority of older adults continued to shudder at the prospect of retirement; their sense of self was intricately tied to their work identity and to their daily interactions in the workplace. But for the most part, people were clearly looking quite favorably on the idea of eventual retirement, for they were voting with their feet by leaving the workforce as soon as they possibly could. When a slightly reduced Social Security pension became available to those leaving the workforce a few years before age sixty-five, social scientists noticed that the average age of retirement began to drop almost simultaneously. Some older adults—those who had accumulated the necessary financial resources—were even choosing to retire in their mid- or late fifties.

Still others were "retiring" in their fifties because their jobs had been eliminated during company downsizing or by mega-mergers, which were on the rise from the 1980s onward. As these mature job seekers tried to return to the marketplace, they often faced difficulties in finding comparable employment, for younger workers were willing to accept lower salaries. Then again, some "retirees" were being forced to accept employee "buyouts," because these offers came with an implicit threat that if a large cash payment was not accepted on the spot, their pension plans (and the company itself) might not be there for them in the future. The company mergers and employee "buyouts" that have been a feature of the late 1990s and early twenty-first century have made these surprisingly early retirements more and more commonplace.

For the most part, though, the average age of retirement for Americans now hovers around sixty-two (though some researchers have seen signs that it may be on the rise again). And in general, most people regard this "third age" of life as a time to anticipate with pleasure—the pot of golden freedom from the strictures of career and family responsibilities that awaits one at the end of life's toils.

According to David Ekerdt, who is director of the Gerontology Center at the University of Kansas, many people now spend a lifetime carefully saving up and mapping out financial plans for the liberated existence they will one day enjoy. As Ekerdt has written: "The thrumming message about retirement planning assumes that retirement is the inevitable destination of a work career. . . . Much like a journey that is dominated by thoughts of the destination, retirement seems to be morphing from just another of life's stages into the place where adulthood arrives." In other words, retirement isn't just a *period* of adulthood; it is adulthood's major goal.

I might add that the messages currently being beamed from the media have underscored this super-positive view of the retirement years. Advertisements from financial planners, which are presently everywhere—on TV and in many magazines—depict retirement as a time for leisure, travel, adventure, fun and self-indulgence. The concluding period of a person's working life is no longer seen as a brief station on the way to the end of his or her existence. Quite the opposite, for an individual who leaves the workplace at sixty-five can live up to twenty-plus years—frequently healthy years—in the role of a retiree. As a result of this and other social forces, as Ekerdt has observed, saving up for retirement has now become "adulthood's great project of deferred gratification."

PHASING OUT

Early on in my initial interview with the Winstons, I introduced the subject of retirement. Was it on their minds? And if so, what were their thoughts about it? These questions brought a somewhat rueful smile to Steve's face, and he told me that until about four years ago, the notion of eventually retiring had not even been on his radar screen.

"Four years or longer, but yes," Jackie said thoughtfully.

Without responding to this comment, Steve went on to say that he hadn't been able to conceive of himself in any way other than working with his patients in his medical practice. "Over the last few years, though, I've developed a strong interest in film—both foreign and independent movies. Not really mainstream, but I see a lot of movies; I rent a lot of movies, and sometimes I even write reviews and send them to a few of our friends. We also go to film festivals. We went to Sundance a couple of years ago. That was a sixtieth-birthday present for me. We went to that with two other couples." A contented expression crossed the physician's face, and he shrugged briefly, then continued.

"Another thing is that I actually used to be scared by the thought of being alone, and wondering how I would spend my time after retiring. Would I go nuts? Would I . . . ?" He shrugged again, leaving the sentence unfinished.

I nodded, smiled and prompted him by saying, " 'Who would I be if there were no colleagues around and no patients waiting in the waiting room?' "

"Exactly right," Steve responded. "But for the last four or five years I've become much more comfortable with myself, and since we've moved into this new community, everyone around here is retired. I mean, *I have friends.*"

He smiled broadly, looked at his wife, who said promptly, "And he's *raving* about it. The men here are all raving about it."

I turned to Jackie and reminded her that in a phone conversation before this meeting she'd said that she had found her situation in the Belmont house "isolating" now that the children had gone. Although she'd continued to see clients in her home occasionally, this had happened only intermittently.

Jackie nodded her agreement, then explained that her office situation in downtown Boston remained unchanged, and she still spent three days a week there. "What *has* changed is our living situation, because there are people all around us now. We're in a *neighborhood.* Which is a very vital thing," she said enthusiastically.

"Yes, for both of us," Steve said. "So we have our old friends from the city, and the new friends we've made in the condominium association. Which is great. For instance, I took a walk with Charlie today, and I could go with Gus tomorrow to play some tennis. So retirement doesn't scare me; not at all, anymore. I might not be happy when I'm fully retired, but I don't feel I would be panicked about it. If I was, I could always do something about it—do something completely different, if I wanted to."

It seemed clear that this relocation had been an extremely happy choice for both of them. I did note some strained feelings on Jackie's part—made evident in fleeting facial expressions rather than in words—that never actually emerged during this first interview. In our follow-up talks a year later, though, her ambivalence about their situation did rise to the surface. Then, she spoke about feeling under a lot of strain due to "having one foot in the world of retirement and one foot in the world of work."

Everyone around them was fully retired, while they themselves were still phasing out. In a way, you could say that they were practicing for what their lives would be like when they left the world of work behind. Still, during this first interview, my belief was that the Winstons' choice had been an unambiguously positive one. I was impressed by the benefits that moving into this new community had accorded them.

"A move like this is a huge decision?" I said, ending my statement on a questioning note.

Both members of the pair nodded in energetic agreement. "It takes *years* of talking," Jackie said. "We'd been thinking about it for a long time—when we would move, when we would downsize." Finally, it was the exemplar of her oldest, closest friend Emily—someone she'd first met at summer camp when they were both seven years old—who'd helped them to make up their minds. Emily and her husband had not only facilitated the Winstons' decision but also eased the newcomers' entry into the closely bonded new friendship group to which they themselves belonged.

Given that the real estate market in Boston and surrounding areas had skyrocketed during the Winstons' years in Belmont, they'd been able to trade in their suburban home for two condominiums. One was in the adult-oriented village where they now lived, and one was in a somewhat similar complex on the west coast of Florida, which was in the same community where Jackie's aged, ailing father resided. Clearly, an almost bewildering number of changes in the couple's lives was now occurring (and what I didn't realize was that I hadn't yet heard the half of it).

I turned to Jackie and asked how she'd felt about cutting back on her office hours as her husband had done. She blushed slightly, said she had always wondered what she would do without her career; it was such a part of her life. "And the fact is that there are many other things I want to do, but I don't want to let go of the job entirely. I love my colleagues. So I would like to make a shift in my work from where I am still doing professional things but without the huge responsibilities."

"She would also miss the income," Steve put in dryly.

Jackie laughed, turned a shade pinker. "I would miss the income," she admitted. Then she went on to say that her husband would have been satisfied with a smaller unit in the condominium association in which they were now living, but she'd insisted on one of the roomier ones. "He would have been fine with the kitchen with the Formica counter, too, but I said, 'No, I'm gutting the kitchen.' My approach is okay. I will work longer so I can do—or we can do—the things that matter to me."

"And I'm more interested in challenges," Steve said. "Things outside the medical field. As far as medicine is concerned, I've been there, done that. . . . And psychologically, I'm ready to move on."

"You want to find other parts of yourself, things you may have left behind?" I asked, my tone speculative.

"Yes, exactly." He paused, thought for a moment, then added, "Or even do things *within* medicine, but outside the context of patient care."

"Which has become repetitive after a while?" I asked.

Steve agreed, but added that direct contact with patients had always made him nervous. "I've never outgrown the nervousness. There's always that unpredictable element—the thing that you don't recognize on the basis of what you're looking at. You just can't predict it! So someone you're sure is fine turns out to be very sick . . . or is sick the next day. And unfortunately—or fortunately, because it keeps you very diligent . . . Still, I've never gotten over those feelings of agita. You send someone home and you think, 'Is *this* going to be the one?' Maybe not in so many words, but you do wonder."

Nevertheless, he said, he still continued to enjoy working with students, whom he often took into his office. These were medical students and physician's-assistant students from various universities who would spend weeks or even months at a time in his office. He also liked working with nurses, teaching them about diseases circulating in the community, "explaining why we treat this disease a certain way, and that disease another way," he said.

"Yes, he does that on his lunchtime," Jackie volunteered.

Steve smiled. "Yes, but I'm still seeing patients . . . though the moneymaking part doesn't interest me. . . . Don't misunderstand, I like the idea of making money. But I don't like the idea of working for it anymore. I used to love it, but I don't love it anymore."

The Winstons had come to a point in their lives where they clearly had enough resources to live on, and to enjoy a very comfortable retirement. Steve had spoken of several different things he would like to do with his time: of his deepening interest in film; of his spending "friendship time" rather than "collegial time" with male buddies; of the gratification he received from supervising medical personnel at different levels of the health care system.

I turned to Jackie with a questioning tilt of my head and said, "How about you? Steve has talked about some other ways of spending his time—movies and film festivals, for instance—that are more playful, more stimulating, more enjoyment-oriented. Do you, too, see a similar aspect of yourself coming into focus right now? I mean, some ways that you'd like to spend your time that are completely *unlike* your work as an architect . . . or perhaps some offshoot from it?"

Jackie leaned forward in her seat. "Yes, yes, I do. First of all, I love drawing and acrylic painting. Secondly, I love photography. My kids have always joked about all the pictures I take! So I want to get further along with all these interests, to learn more about them. I've already signed up for a drawing class which is starting in the fall."

"So each of you is saying that you'd like to do more with the creative, playful parts of yourself at this point in time?" I asked them.

The partners turned to each other, smiled and turned back to me. "Yes," they said in unison, and that made them laugh aloud.

Jackie went on to say that she, too, enjoyed mentoring younger people in her field. She also donated her time for certain causes, particularly cancer causes that she felt strongly about. "I want to do things that are worthwhile—give back. I really *care* about people," she said.

Steve was interested in volunteering, too. He gave his time and financial support to a handful of his favorite charitable organizations, and at present, he was running for a seat on the board of one of them. "Give *back* . . . That's exactly what I said to Jackie. People reach our age and they say, 'Oh my God, how can I help other people?'"

I grew quiet for a few moments, thinking of psychoanalyst Erik Erikson's description of that crisis of adult growth that he defined as "generativity versus stagnation." Erikson spoke of generativity as a stage of increasing creativity and altruism—manifested by a growing concern for future generations and for the human community in general. A person who has successfully navigated this developmental passage was someone who would enjoy imparting his or her skills and wisdom to others less knowledgeable and experienced. He did so because he *cared* about others, in the most general sense of that word. And now, looking at the Winstons, it seemed to me that when it came to generativity, this couple was a model example of what Erickson meant.

CHANGES

In recent years, these partners had experienced a huge life speedup, as though their settled lives had suddenly started moving on fast-forward. Jackie discovered her precancerous condition, and then Steve experienced his episode of transient global amnesia. During this same period, the Winstons put their Belmont house on the market.

That project had involved a lot of redecoration, because their home needed to be repainted and restored to meet more contemporary tastes. Jackie had taken charge of this project, plus that of figuring out what furniture to keep, sell or send to the new condo in Florida. Then their daughter-in-law and oldest son had a baby—their first grandchild. Shortly afterward, their second son announced his engagement, and the young couple married the following summer. The Winstons were very close to both sons, and to their daughters-in-law as well.

Then, in the midst of all these events, Jackie's father had become very ill and been hospitalized. "So I had all these house redecorations going on while my father was with us for six weeks," Jackie related. "And he was great—he was fabulous, my dad. At the same time, Steve was taking care of all the paperwork and the lawyers on the real estate, but he was also running back and forth to the hospital, supervising the doctors who were caring for my father. I don't think my father would be *alive* if Steve hadn't taken charge in that way, constantly supervising his care." She shot a grateful glance at her husband. "My dad got better, and he went back to Florida after about eight weeks."

"So many things happening so fast," I said. "It sounds like a Marx Brothers movie."

They laughed, and Steve said, "All of that was going on, plus we've had a lot of social things going on in our new place. People invite us to parties, and we want to be with them, to make friends. Even though we're working, we've been going out a couple of times during the week, which is something we never used to do. But now we usually have a quick dinner with a friend on Monday night, and then go to a movie with a friend. On Wednesday night, we go out, and often on Thursday and Friday night, too. And on the weekend we go out, or we visit the kids. So we've literally not had that much time together . . . whether casual time or intimate time."

I smiled, amused. I couldn't help but think of one of the formerly most accepted theories of aging, the one called "disengagement." This had to do with the belief that as people become older, they begin to withdraw emotionally. They do so because they feel devitalized, unable to offer much to anyone, in either old or new relationships. And with the passage of time, as their affect continued to flatten, they continued disengaging from everyone around them.

The Winstons, I thought, were hardly disengaged. Now in their early sixties, they seemed to have about as much social life as—or more than—they could possibly handle.

THE SUBTLY INHIBITING FACTOR

We were drawing to the end of the interview. *"What do you think are the major sexual issues that emerge at this time of life?"* I asked the pair.

There was a silence, and then Jackie asked, "Now versus before?"

I nodded. "Now versus earlier." She didn't reply, but turned to Steve, asked, "What do you think?"

He raised an eyebrow. "Very good, Jackie. That was *good*," he said dryly. He turned to me, smiled. "She's good at tossing the ball." They started laughing.

Then, in a voice grown serious, Jackie said, "You know what it is—we've been *harried*. Neither of us wants to . . . to do anything. We're affectionate, we're very affectionate with each other. That part hasn't changed."

"Right," said her spouse.

"But in terms of sex, the appetite has . . ." Jackie's voice trailed off. Steve came to her rescue, saying, "Also, about four years ago, I started taking Paxil."

I wondered why he had begun taking Paxil, which, like Prozac, is commonly used to treat depression. "Were you depressed at the time?" I asked him.

Steve said that no, he had never been depressed; he began taking it for anxiety. Actually, he said, he had begun taking it during a period of time when a lot of people were using that medication for anxiety. "And I found that it really did help. It helped a *lot*. But one of the side effects is that over time, libido will shrink."

I nodded, said I knew that Paxil (which is one of the selective serotonin reuptake inhibitors, or SSRIs) could have deadly side effects when it came to sexual performance. But when I said so, Steve told me that in his own case it actually *wasn't* deadly when it came to the performance aspects of sex.

"However, it's certainly cut down on my libido," he acknowledged, adding quickly, "I mean, it's cut down, but it's not dead." His voice had dropped and become softer, as if he were afraid an outsider might be listening.

What came to my mind at that moment was the way he'd described his obsessive worrying about each patient he saw: *Is this the one? Have I made a faulty diagnosis?* However, what I said aloud was, "Do you think the Paxil is worth it to you? Considering its side effects?"

Steve said that this was a matter he'd been turning over in his mind that very morning. Because it wasn't only the sexual problem; he'd also been experiencing a deep sense of fatigue. "I've been so much more tired lately—unusual for me—and I've been wondering if that has something to do with the drug. So it's a combination of things. And I've been thinking I may need to revisit this whole issue." He was so much more de-energized than he recalled ever being.

Jackie hadn't been sleeping well, either, she said. She'd been trying to bring order to everything that was going on—in terms of the move, her father's illness, the birth of their grandson, the marriage of their other son, the effort to integrate themselves into the new community—and remained awake making endless lists of things that needed to be done. Fortunately, the sleep problem had eased up recently, but she believed that to some degree she'd been sleepwalking through the past couple of years.

"And as far as sex goes," Steve said, "we have just not had that much *time*. Okay, we could have made a pact that every Monday night we are going to be in the sack, but we just haven't done that."

I shrugged, said it sounded as if it wasn't creating a problem for either of them—or a problem between them. "Maybe this is a period when you both need to back off, for some reason or another?" I floated the question.

This did not sit well with either of the Winstons. "No, no, I think we need to work on it," Jackie protested immediately. I shrugged, said they didn't need to work on it if neither of them was feeling deprived, and Steve said quickly, "I want to work on it."

"That makes two of us," Jackie said at once.

What, then, was standing in their way? I asked them if they had ever tried Viagra, but Steve reminded me that he had no problems with performance issues. "It's just getting the interest up. It's libido, only libido."

I turned to Jackie, talked about how it often happens that when one member of a pair loses sexual interest, the other one's level of desire begins to wane as well. She nodded, said she thought that was true of them, but there were other things involved too. "I think I just can't get interested," she stated evenly. "I feel very affectionate toward Steve, very loving. But I'm not missing anything. I'm just not missing it."

I asked them, then, about their general level of frequency; they said they had intercourse about once every ten days. I found this particular number a highly doubtful one, but merely said this wasn't out of the normal range at their stage of life.

For a brief space of time, neither of the Winstons said anything. "I think it's the *quality*, rather than the quantity, that we're feeling," Jackie said finally, in a candid, definitive tone of voice.

What flashed into my mind at that moment were the three activities the Winstons had been told might bring on another episode of transient global amnesia: the first one was long drives alone in the car, the second was swimming in cold water and the third one was sexual activity. Was fear of a recurrence the subtly inhibiting factor that neither one of the couple was consciously thinking, much less talking openly with the other about?

Chapter Seven

JACKIE AND STEVE WINSTON (2)

RETIREMENT MYTHS,

RETIREMENT REALITIES

There is probably no more persistent folk belief than the idea that the person who leaves the busy, buzzing social world of the workplace will experience a deterioration in physical health shortly thereafter. Even though well-researched findings dating back to the 1950s point in the *opposite* direction, the notion that retirement often leads directly to illness (or to death) keeps recurring in the popular and at times even the medical and scientific literature.

What makes this myth of aging so difficult to dislodge? For one thing, many of the anecdotes that circulate among friends, relatives and colleagues serve to supply a wealth of seemingly supportive evidence. Everyone has heard the familiar story of someone who retired at sixty-seven, then died suddenly of a heart attack six months later. Naturally, we tend to assign a cause-and-effect theory to our understanding of that individual's sudden decline and passing.

However, what often goes unnoticed is the state of that person's health *before* retiring—indeed, we don't know whether or not he or she retired because of a preexisting heart disease. Actually, one-fourth of retirees do choose to leave the workplace due to an illness or disability, so if a sick individual's health continues its downward course over time, it can't be ascribed to the retirement decision itself. That person's physical state would have been likely to continue its decline whether he or she had remained in the workplace or not.

Furthermore, the retiree may have gotten much sicker even sooner if the work environment was hostile, or if the heavy demands of the job was a source of remorseless pressure. However, since retirement is one of later adulthood's major life transitions, we tend to assume that any physical or emotional problem that someone suffers afterward is due to the stress of transitioning from the life that was to the one that will be lived in the future.

The tenacity of the conviction that retirement is a threat to health—in the face of over half a century's contravening evidence—may, on the other hand, be due to our society's deep-seated commitment to the work ethic. "Negative views of retirement are consistent with the cultural ideology that celebrates work as the source of self-worth, self-esteem, identity and personal fulfillment," David Ekerdt has written. "People can say disparaging things about retirement and health to defend their own commitment to work. . . ."

Whatever the underlying reasons, the idea that continues to be recycled is that remaining in the economic marketplace keeps you vital and healthy, and that you leave the world of work at your own physical and emotional peril. Everyone appears to "know" that working and retirement are the inverse of each other, and that the former keeps you hale and hardy, while the latter leads to slow deterioration and impending death.

EVIDENCE TO THE CONTRARY

Until the 1980s, the numerous studies reporting that retirement has no adverse effects on physical well-being were in the nature of self-report studies. This research is inevitably affected by the ambiguities of different types of research criteria as well as with fairly crude indicators such as incidence of disease and mortality figures.

But in the early 1980s, four investigators—David Ekerdt, Lynn Baden, Raymond Bosse and Elaine Dibbs—carried out a careful study comparing the pre- and post-retirement changes in physical health among men who had retired and their age peers who remained in the workplace. This was the first study that followed a large sample of men over time, scrupulously comparing the health of those who had retired with those who continued working. Given that the men were all in the same age range (between fifty-five and seventy-three), would one group's health look different from the other's?

The participants in this research were all part of a much larger group (two thousand men) taking part in the Veterans Administration Normative Aging Study, a Boston-based longitudinal study that has been ongoing since 1963. The men who made up the Ekerdt et al. sample were selected from the larger bloc and consisted of subjects who were (1) in relatively good health; (2) were likely to remain in the local area; and (3) came from a diverse range of backgrounds and educational levels.

All subjects in the Normative Aging Study received extensive medical examinations every five years up until the age of fifty-two, and every three years thereafter. The group of retirees included in the Ekerdt research was selected on the basis of their age and date of retirement (if they had retired) as well as their results in the ongoing

Normative Aging Study medical examinations. These included the individual's medical history and continuing physical examinations by an internist, including an ECG, chest X-ray and standard blood and urine tests. A registered nurse also rated the individual's physical health along a 4-point scale.

The RN doing the medical rating was blind to whether the person was retired or still working, and also whether he was being rated at Time 1 (the beginning of a four-year time span) or Time 2 (four years after his initial medical status had been determined).

The results of this study were unequivocal. Men who had retired were no less healthy than their peers who were still working. Moreover, even if the person had retired due to compulsory age rules or under other stressful circumstances, such as a company buyout, his health status did not suffer. The Ekerdt researchers concluded that "the findings from this prospective study indicated that the experience of health changes over three to four years among men who were employed and then retired did not significantly differ from health changes among age peers who remained at work." These findings have never been disproved, and yet the prevailing belief that retirement leads to a speedily declining health status continues to persist.

Perhaps such underlying concerns were part of an unspoken worry that kept Dr. Steve Winston and his wife, Jackie, in a virtually unchanged position a year later. For when I came to do my follow-up interviews with them, they were both still putting in a full three-day workweek, though surrounded by neighbors who were fully retired. It was as though they had waded just so far into the waters of the world beyond work but were hesitant to immerse themselves completely.

To be sure, it is true that the course they were following was not a particularly unusual one. Retirement is no longer viewed as the cutoff point of a linear working career—so that one day you are a fully employed person who is present on the job, and the next day you disappear from the world of work forever. On the contrary, the current retirement role is more along the lines of a cyclical living and learning and working model, in which periods of leisure and of taking courses (literature, cooking, mathematics) are interspersed with periods of flexible working arrangements, such as part-time or seasonal employment. Volunteer projects are also part of this mix, so that lifelong engagement—in various jobs or other activities—has been steadily replacing the traditional notion of retirement as a time of withdrawal and rocking on the porch in a state of increasing social withdrawal. At present, the retired person's role is no longer so rigidly circumscribed as it was, say, in the period of the 1950s. Now it is a role that requires designing and customizing by the retiree him- or herself.

SEX AND TRANSIENT GLOBAL AMNESIA

Before this follow-up meeting, Jackie had e-mailed me to say "things had changed" and implied that she wasn't finding them too easy. On this occasion, we were meeting in the Winstons' handsome, well-furnished condominium, which was located in a woodsy, well-ordered housing complex. As usual, I was planning to interview each one of them separately, but initially we spent a short while together.

It was mid-January, and we each held a mug of hot tea in hand. I began by asking Jackie in what ways things had changed. For a moment she looked at me blankly. "Did I say things had changed?" she asked. She seemed perplexed. "I don't really know. What's true is that I'm feeling highly ambivalent, so maybe that was coming through. I feel like it's hard to live in a retirement community when you're still working. Even though we've both cut down to three days a week, I sometimes feel like I'm working full-time. I see clients, and then I come home and work on my designs. I do other things for the office, even on my day off—things that have to be done to keep a private firm running. And I've been invited into a book club in this community, and I play bridge once a week . . . so it's hard keeping up. I've had a couple of dinner parties, too, so people won't think we're stand-offish, but it's *hard*. I feel a lot of pressure because we're trying to be a part of the neighborhood here, and at the same time I'm still putting a lot of energy into my work."

I recalled that in our last interview Steve had complained about going out on weeknights, when their former custom had been to socialize on weekends only. I asked him if he felt as pressured as his wife did.

Steve shook his head. "No, I don't. I'm not sure why. Probably it's because I'm not putting as much energy into my work as Jackie is. We both put in the same number of workdays, but I sold my practice to my partners just before we met with you last year."

He added with a pleased smile, "Now I'm no longer the boss."

I asked him if he had the same worried feeling every time a patient left—the anxiety about having made a wrong diagnosis.

A year had passed, and Steve didn't recall ever telling me that; but he acknowledged that these kinds of feelings hadn't changed. "I'm still always concerned about it; that has never eased off. Which is what makes me so thorough in what I do. I take it enormously seriously."

"Did you stay on the Paxil?" I asked. He shook his head, saying that he had quit taking the drug for three months and found himself growing more and more anxious. "So I went for a consultation in New York City with a neuropsychiatrist. I then decided to start taking Celexa, which I'm taking now. That's been fine, and I'm not anxious. But this drug doesn't seem to have the same negative effect on libido."

"Really? I suppose that—" I started to say, but Steve interrupted quickly. "To get back to what we were talking about before—I don't share Jackie's experience about feeling pressure."

He was grabbing the basketball of the conversation out of my hands and running down the court in the opposite direction. So I began to talk about having reviewed the first audiotapes I had made with them and noting the symptoms that might bring on another episode of transient global amnesia. "You said that one thing that could cause a problem is the monotony of driving alone . . . ?" I asked Steve.

"I probably did say that, yes," he replied.

"You said that sex was another thing," I went on, and he nodded yes.

"So does that have a scary effect when you guys have sex?" I asked, my tone hesitant, looking from one member of the couple to the other.

Steve shook his head. "No, no, not at all," he said. And Jackie said quickly, "Probably that's because it's when you're with me, and you're not alone."

Steve laughed. "I don't have sex when I'm not with you."

We all laughed, and Jackie said wryly, "That's good. I meant that you're not driving alone."

"Nice try, Jackie," her husband said affectionately, and Jackie admitted that she might be a bit off today; she hadn't slept very well the night before.

RELOCATING: THE RIGHT DECISION?

My separate interviews with each member of the couple followed their typical preordained course. I make use of a questionnaire adapted from the Grant Study, which is a longitudinal study of Harvard and Pennsylvania University graduates, tracking the course of their lives over time. However, it must be said that I always give this set of questions my own spin, spending more time on questions that seem more fruitful in a particular case, and passing quickly over those that appear to be of little relevance. I've also added a couple of questions of my own.

I began by asking Jackie in what ways her relationship with Steve had changed over time.

She took a sip of tea, then stared down into the cup for a few moments. "It feels a lot like we're going into a new stage," she said at last. "In a couple of years we'll retire. I'll probably work a bit, or maybe I won't work at all. And maybe Steve will work, too—at medicine, or at something else. But I'm unsure about what it will feel like—being retired. First of all, there's the financial difference: when we both worked, I had a housekeeper. She came in twice a week, and when I had a dinner party, she made some of the dishes for it. She would do the main dish, and I would do a side thing and the salad. Then she'd tidy up afterward, so having people over was not a big deal."

Over the years, Jackie had gotten out of the habit of doing any serious cooking, so she was having to learn how to entertain without the same reliable assistance. "It becomes stressful in terms of wanting to do things in a certain way—and I think my own perfectionism is part of the pressure. So I get agitated, and Steve is not great around the house. I mean, he is a great guy, and he does a lot of things . . . takes care of the bills. But when it comes to keeping up with the way the place looks, or getting ready for a dinner party . . ." She shrugged her shoulders.

"It's your job," I said, and she nodded.

"Yes, it's my job, and I don't have the energy I had years ago. So the anxiety I'm feeling is about being able to do all the social things—the pressures to become part of the community. I mean, I haven't played bridge in forever, so here it is again. We took lessons with some other couples, and so that's one thing. Then there's the tennis: we've gotten back into tennis, and I actually hurt myself doing that. So it's sort of retooling some of these skills that I haven't been interested in for years. I don't feel as if I have to be *better* than other people at bridge or tennis—just good enough to be part of the group, to be connected." Jackie's face wore a worried, somewhat guilty expression.

Then she added hastily that in many ways she was finding it wonderful to be in this new community, and that they'd made friends they liked very much already. "Some people we've met are really lovely," she repeated, but then added that other groups among the residents were constantly having parties, and then she and Steve had to invite them back. "And it's just a *lot*. I do feel as if I still have a job, even though I'm in the office only three days a week. And I still *like* my work. But it takes a lot of energy if you pile it on the energy you need for these other things, too."

"You do sound like you're running on all cylinders," I said sympathetically. "I see you as someone in a transitional time. And someone who's finding the transition hard."

Jackie nodded, said haltingly, "I do feel it . . . that it's a transition that would probably be stressful for anyone. But if you're working at a job you love, it's even harder."

I smiled, observed that she didn't seem to have just a foot, but one whole *leg*, in her work life and the other leg in the life of a retired person—and they seemed to be splitting apart.

"That's right," Jackie said, looking pleased that I seemed to understand. She grew silent for a short while, then said thoughtfully that though she was glad they'd left their big house in Belmont, with all the upkeep and its large lawn, she still wasn't sure it had made sense to do so while they were still working people. Moreover, she and Steve had found themselves to be among the youngest residents of the condominium complex.

"Most of these people moved here when they were our age, twenty years ago. By and large, the people here are much older than we are." She sighed. "I'm not sure what the answer is."

"About relocating?" I asked her.

"Exactly," she said. "It's not that it was a bad idea to leave the house when we did. But if you're doing it a few years before retiring, it's tremendously stressful."

It occurred to me that the Winstons had made the decision to downsize because of two health scares: Jackie's breast cancer fright and Steve's unnerving episode of transient global amnesia. But neither of them had been truly ready to depart from his or her original career. It was as if doing so would be too risky—a form of giving up and giving in that might initiate a downhill slide in terms of their emotional and physical well-being. So as things stood, Jackie had found herself in a kind of age ghetto, where her life was in part committed to an absorbing career she still cherished and therefore differed significantly from the lives of her much older neighbors.

A TRIGGER OF FEAR

I was talking with Jackie alone. "When you're upset emotionally, or sad, or worried about something that has nothing to do with Steve, what do you do? Do you go to him, or do you go to someone else, or what do you do?"

Jackie didn't hesitate. "I go to Steve."

"And how does he respond?"

She looked uncertain. "You mean, when I complain to him?"

I nodded, asked her what usually happened next. Did he listen?

Jackie smiled. "Oh yes, yes. He's a very good listener. But sometimes he'll bring in a thought about how to handle a situation that makes me feel like I'm not being understood. So I'll say, 'Hey, wait a minute, I don't think you get it.' We are very out there when it comes to getting things straight between us."

"Are there concerns or problems you don't usually discuss with him?"

"No, no," Jackie said, with a dismissive wave of her hand. "Steve is my best friend."

"What do you do if he's upset, emotionally."

Jackie paused, took a sip of tea, replaced the cup on the coffee table between us. "When Steve is upset about something, he becomes . . . quiet. Sometimes it will take me a while to figure out what's wrong."

"And then will you ask him about it? And is he able to tell you?" I asked.

She nodded an unambiguous yes to both questions, and I laughed, said that in my experience men often have trouble looking inside their own heads. Jackie laughed, too, and said that her husband was definitely introspective. "He'll say what's going on, and I'll pay attention, and in some instances, I'll get pretty worked up. That happens in situations where I think he should be angry or upset with someone, but he just isn't. He'll tell me the whole story as if he has no feelings about it whatsoever—and then *I'm* the one who gets angry! Then he gets mad at me, and says that's not being helpful. So that's something that happens between us."

I smiled, said that perhaps she *was* being helpful—perhaps she was being the voice of his anger. Jackie smiled wryly. "Oh, he can argue," she said, but then added pacifically, "But I can also get too wound up, as you can see."

"How have the ups and downs in his health affected your relationship?"

"I'm not really sure," Jackie said carefully. "It's left me feeling I have to keep tabs on him a little bit. It's been a concern for me. And sometimes when he forgets something and I say, 'Don't you remember that happening?' I can see that he gets scared. So, when that happens, which is not a big deal in and of itself, it feels like it's some sort of trigger for him."

She was silent for a few moments, then said, "You know, I think that there is some sort of post-traumatic stress reaction that pertains to anything involving memory. When he realizes he's forgotten something, he'll try and try to bring the word or incident to mind. I myself don't think there's anything wrong with his memory, but this is a scenario that does keep getting played out."

"What's the most important thing you've learned from knowing Steve? And what do you think is the most important thing he's learned from knowing you?"

These questions seemed to confound Jackie. She sat across from me, frowning perplexedly. "The most important thing I've learned about myself or about life?" she asked, finally.

Puzzled by her bafflement, I shrugged, said, "Whatever comes to mind."

A silence ensued, and at last I broke it off by saying, "Let's move on if that question doesn't work for you."

She shook her head, nonplussed. "I'm just not . . . nothing special is coming to me."

"How about Steve?" I asked. "What's the most important thing he's learned from knowing you?"

"You'd have to ask him," Jackie replied, one eyebrow arching skyward.

I laughed, said, "Okay, I will."

Then, as if out of nowhere, she said, "Marriage is not unconditional love." Unsure of what she meant by this cryptic remark, I shook my head as if to say I wasn't following.

Jackie asked me if I knew what the term "alexithymic" referred to. I paused, said I thought it meant the inability to experience or express emotion. I waited for her to continue, and after a few moments, she said that her mother had been like that—unable to show tenderness or affection to either her or her younger brother. Then, as if to justify her mother's failure to connect to her babies, Jackie explained that her parent's own early life had been bleak—she'd been orphaned by age eleven, and this grim early history had left her fearful of relating to anyone.

"To truly love could be to truly lose," I murmured, and she nodded. "She was too frightened, I believe," Jackie said. Tears sprang to her eyes and disappeared immediately.

We continued with the interview then, and toward its close I asked her, *What have been the best things about being in this marriage?* Jackie replied that it was what we had talked about earlier—having a best friend for life. "Steve's my best friend, and we have a lot in common—

a lot of things we both love doing together. We both love movies, drama, ballet, travel. We just have a lot of joint interests, which is nice . . . to share these things." It occurred to me, then, that while Jackie Winston had not experienced unconditional love in her earliest years, it was in her marriage that she had come closest to it.

Finally, at the close of the interview I asked her what word or phrase she would use to describe this particular phase of her life.

"Adjustment," she said at once, then paused and added, "Transitional."

Is Sex a Concern?

I was interviewing Steve alone.

"Aging affects many aspects of life, including sex life. Has yours changed?" I asked him. "I guess we talked about this earlier." During my conversation with Jackie, I had asked her the same question, and she'd indicated that the change from Paxil to Celexa had pretty much brought their sexual life back to its previous state. But Steve said otherwise. "I don't think that anything has really changed since we saw you a year ago," he said frankly.

Even though Celexa was not the same as Paxil in terms of its damping effect on his libido, there hadn't been much change as far as their sexual activity was concerned. Their sex life had fallen off markedly in the past five to ten years, and in Steve's opinion, the libido issue was a part—but not all—of the problem. "Even though it's much better with this medication that I'm taking now, there hasn't been any noticeable improvement in our sex life," he said.

Jackie had surely intimated otherwise, but I didn't feel surprised by her doing so. I think there is such deep shame connected with not

being as sexually responsive or as sexually active as one or both partners thinks they ought to be. Moreover, if people hold the yardstick of
their earlier years against their older years—and don't have flexible
criteria with which to evaluate the quality, frequency and nature of
their sexual experience—they will feel a sense of embarrassment and
failure. Even though they may take changes in memory or energy or
stamina in stride, they feel that their sexual appetites ought to be
unchanged.

"Is this a concern for one of you, or both of you, right now?" I
asked, hesitantly.

"I don't think we have enough sex, and I think Jackie would agree
with that," Steve said.

"Does somebody feel that he or she would like to have sex more
often?" I ventured.

"Yes," Steve said forthrightly. He seemed unfazed.

"Who?" I asked.

He laughed. "Jackie and Steve," he replied. Then his expression
grew serious. "We both feel we would like to have more. We're both
unhappy about what's not happening."

This was so at odds with what Jackie had told me earlier. "Does this
mean that *both* of you are unhappy about this?" I realized that I was
parroting what he had just told me, and he must have, too, for he simply nodded.

I thought about the other couples I'd interviewed (such as the
Donaldsons) who'd voiced grievances about their diminished sexual
activities, but who weren't basically dissatisfied with the situation as it
existed. "People often compare their present-day sex lives with the
way it was early in the relationship," I said. "Then the drop-off—
which isn't different from so many other aspects of aging, such as

energy levels and physical strength—makes them feel miserable about themselves."

Steve shrugged. "I don't know. I'm not satisfied with things as they are. And when I talk to Jackie, she says she isn't satisfied, either."

I smiled. "So why don't two people who are not satisfied . . . ?"

Steve smiled. "Do something about it?" Then he shrugged again, said he didn't know, and that I would have to tune in tomorrow. "We tend to be exhausted at night, and we just don't find the time. It's not that we watch television; we don't. But in the evening—if we're at home—I'm usually catching up on patient notes and Jackie's working on her sketches and designs. So, before we know it, we're both exhausted and we fall into bed and just go to sleep."

I smiled, said, "You both say, 'Gee, we should be having sex more often,' and then turn over and go to sleep."

Steve laughed, said that I'd made a good point. "You have two people who don't disagree, so what the hell is the problem?" Starting today, he added, things were going to change. "The children are out of the house, this is the time of our lives," he stated. But then he told me that they also had a grandchild now, who occupied a lot of their time. They went down to Stamford to visit with the family every four to six weeks. "We babysit for her, and it's been great. It's just delightful," he said.

Steve and Jackie Winston were a very busy, warm, deeply engaged couple. I wondered if they would continue being too busy for their intimate sexual life.

WHAT I LEARNED FROM HER

"Are your arguments any different than they used to be?" I had asked the Winstons this question in my earlier interview, and they had looked at each other questioningly, half smiles on their faces.

Finally, Steve had said he didn't think so. Their quarrels were always about Jackie's perfectionism—her high standards when it came to keeping the house neat and clean, and her need to entertain in a flawless way. Jackie said that once, at a large holiday dinner, Steve brought additional turkey stuffing to the table in an ordinary mixing bowl. Jackie was appalled. The beauty of her table—the carefully arranged china, the glinting silver and delicate glassware—had been blighted when that crude dish was plunked down in the midst of everything.

Now, when I asked this question of Steve once again, he told me that this fact of their lives hadn't changed. When they got into arguments it was always about the same thing—keeping the house immaculate, as if royal visitors might pop in for a visit at any minute.

"How has your relationship changed over time, do you think?" was my next question.

Steve pondered this issue briefly. "I think that as we've gotten older I've become more mellow and capable of understanding Jackie in a far more meaningful way. So that I don't take some aspects of her behavior as an insult or a provocation."

"You mean you're less likely to react to her perfectionism?" I asked.

Steve nodded. "I can understand it better now, so I don't take it as a grievous assault in the ways that I did before. I tend to want to please Jackie a lot, and I tend to feel uncomfortable when she's unhappy. It's just the way I am—the way *we* are. I'm much less concerned with what other people are thinking, but in terms of Jackie . . . I just feel miserable when I've made her feel bad. I can't get it out of my mind, and I keep wondering, 'What's she thinking now? What's she thinking now?' But I don't consider it an attack in the way that I did. I'm able to separate us—her needs, my needs—much more than I was able to before."

"So you don't get as upset about something that would have really pissed you off twenty years ago." It was a question, but it emerged as a statement. My thought was that in fact their arguments *had* changed, at least in volume if not in content.

"Correct. I don't take something Jackie says as viscerally as I used to—whereas before I heard it as an assault on my character or some terrible defect of my being. Now I just see it for what it is, at the time when it happens."

"And what is it you see?" I asked.

"It's more on the order of a disagreement. Jackie sees me as being messy. Well, I'm not messy compared to most other men. It's just that our standards are at different levels, and if I don't conform to Jackie's standards, she gets upset. She's not able to tolerate that." He smiled dolefully. "I handle that by saying, 'Just give me a job to do. Because I don't really know how to get the ball in the right place. It just doesn't register for me. So *tell me* what to do.'"

"What's the most important thing you've learned from knowing Jackie? And what do you think is the most important thing she's learned from knowing you?"

Steve didn't hesitate. He said that he didn't think Jackie had ever been really good at seeing how she fit into the world. She didn't know how she fit in with other people, and how other people really saw her. "I think, through me, she's been able to see the positive aspects of her personality. Jackie has a tendency to be down on herself, and that's where her hearing problem has come into it. She thinks that people are going to think she's dumb if she misses part of a conversation. But if she says, 'I'm having trouble hearing' or 'Will you speak a little louder,' there's not a problem. So she's learned to be more up-front about this. . . . But what's most important is that she's able to recognize how other people can and do see her—and I think she's learned that through me." He was telling me, with pride in his voice, that as the person closest to Jackie, he'd been the source of steady corrective feedback.

Steve paused, drew in a deep breath, exhaled and then said, "I would say that the most important thing I've learned from *her* is how to be good. Jackie is the goodest person I know. She just gives everybody a fair shake. She has essentially little, if any, bias. She is just open, very open to ideas; and also, she is very, very loving. And over the years, she's shown me how to be better at loving—with our children and with other people, too—how to be open and honest about my feelings. I think, when I met her, I was a very closed kind of person; I would not discuss my emotions with . . . with anybody. So in this relationship I learned something crucially important: how to open up and do that."

I said that it sounded as if he really admired his wife.

"I do," Steve replied. "I admire Jackie *a lot*. She's just a great person."

Chapter Eight

CLAUDIA AND DOUGLAS HAMILTON

AN UNCERTAIN FUTURE

C laudia Hamilton (then Claudia DeNatale) was a woman I'd interviewed in the late 1970s while doing research for my book *Unfinished Business.* The subject of that work had been the precipitating causes of a depressive disorder at the successive stages of the female life cycle. At that time, I'd listened to the painful story of Claudia's young adulthood, although I had never ended up writing about it.

Now, some thirty years later, I was meeting with Claudia and her husband Douglas in the quiet upstairs office of my home in Hamden, Connecticut. Before describing our three-way discussion, however, let me outline what I already knew about Claudia's earlier life, because it will explain some of the images and memories that kept coming to my mind during the course of the present interview.

Claudia DeNatale had been a twenty-six-year-old divorcée at the time of our first series of meetings. The theme of our conversations had been her long descent into an immobilizing, self-hating, frankly suicidal depression from which it had taken her many months to recover. Claudia, who was in therapy throughout the course of our discussions, said that this severe depression had developed during an eight-year marriage that she portrayed as "thoroughly neglectful, disastrous and abusive." Her husband spent most of his time either working on a small boat he owned or going out drinking with his buddies in the evenings. And when he came home, thoroughly intoxicated, he started barking orders, criticizing her for anything he could think of, and sometimes he even descended to intimidating pushing and shoving. Claudia, who admitted to having an Italian temper of her own, told me that she had found it impossible to defend herself against this person who was taller, stronger and often irrational.

But intolerable as her married life had become, she hadn't seen any way of escaping her situation. Claudia was a good Sicilian daughter, the brightest, most charmed sibling in her family, and leaving her husband would precipitate a scandal in the community that would be humiliating to both herself and her parents. She felt miserable and hopelessly cornered.

Over time, the situation worsened. She found herself spending not only many of her evenings but often full nights alone. Her husband had stopped speaking to her, and wasn't showing up at home very often. So in the early hours of one morning, when the sun had not yet risen, she decided to make use of the lethal concoction of sleeping medications she'd been saving up for just this occasion. Using the logic of the depressive, she'd decided she could not go on with her life.

But then, on an impulse, instead of taking the pills, she looked up the telephone number of the priest of her local parish. Claudia had never met this cleric, for she and her husband didn't go to church. Nevertheless, the priest responded to her hysterical, semicoherent appeal by telling her to get into her car and come to see him immediately.

The young wife, barely coherent, arrived at the rectory in a T-shirt, a pajama top and a pair of old dungarees. Sobbing, she'd collapsed in the pastor's study and then—between tears, complaints and self-recriminations—the story of her marriage to a controlling, tyrannical, belittling, absentee spouse had emerged. To Claudia's surprise, the priest was not critical of her as a "bad wife"; he was tender, kind and understanding. He even suggested that she give thought to the idea of separating from her husband.

Claudia DeNatale was then in her late twenties, but what became clear to me, in the course of our talks, was that she was still struggling with certain core adolescent issues relating to growing up and separating from the family in which she had grown up. These issues revolved, for the most part, around a steamy, vaguely sexualized relationship with her father. Her dad had always favored this "special" daughter, and showed her off to his friends everywhere he went, including his favorite saloon. In fact he treated Claudia like a cute little wife, while treating his real wife with obvious neglect and disrespect.

Not surprisingly, her parents' hostile relationship became the model for the "disastrous" marriage Claudia herself later entered. Yet unlike her mother, who stuck it out through a lifetime—and with the young priest's unfailing sympathy, friendship and advice—Claudia had been able to obtain a separation and divorce from her first husband within a couple of years. This turn of events and her return to her parents' home had—to her surprise—pleased her father enormously. "How often do you get to raise a daughter twice?" he kept asking his relatives and neighbors delightedly.

AN EASYGOING MAN

Today I was sitting down with Claudia DeNatale Hamilton and Douglas Hamilton to discuss their marriage for a book on "couples over fifty." Now, as the partners sat before me, I drew a horizontal line on my sketch pad and asked, "How long have you guys been married?"

At the same time, I was picturing the Claudia I'd known so much earlier. She had been a young woman with wide, frightened-looking hazel eyes and straight dark hair that hung well below her shoulders. I remembered, too, the way in which her story had emerged in gulps, halts and episodes of sobbing. Now she seemed far more self-possessed. Her hair was cut close to her head in a shorter, more no-nonsense way, and she looked plumper and more matronly. Clearly, she was much more at ease with herself. I was picking up none of that electric tension that often set me vibrating, like a violin string, during our long-ago series of conversations.

The partners looked at each other swiftly, questioningly, as if waiting for the other person to answer my question. Then they laughed. "Twenty-five years," Claudia said, turning to me with a smile.

"Twenty-five years," echoed Doug. He, too, was a stolid, somewhat heavily built man. I asked him his age, and he said he was sixty-three, and his wife was one year younger.

It was a second marriage for both of them.

As I was quickly jotting down the important dates relevant to their marital histories, I realized that Claudia must have been in her mid- to late thirties at the time of her remarriage. So she had been single for a decade or more following her separation and divorce.

I asked Doug for the name of his first wife, and he replied in an unwilling tone of voice, "Patti . . . but I don't talk much about that.

That was a pretty rough . . . Patti was a woman with ideas of her own."
He shrugged dismissively.

"Meaning what?" I asked.

"Meaning she was a woman with ideas of her own," he repeated.

"Meaning she was unfaithful?" I asked. He nodded. "Very much so.
Pretty much from the start of the marriage. I was in the military, and I
was never at home, so I probably shouldn't blame her." He made this
statement in an equable tone of voice, but I wondered whether the
sudden flush on his cheeks belied this tolerant statement.

Doug Hamilton was the parent of two sons, Doug Jr., now thirty-
seven, and Gary, thirty-five. I asked him if, considering his ex-wife's
promiscuous behavior, he was sure that both of these young men were
his own biological offspring.

"I know that one is, for sure. The other one is a toss-up," he said,
almost offhandedly.

Claudia leaned forward, placed a hand on his knee. "Oh no, he
isn't. . . . Don't you remember the blood test?" she asked him. She
turned to me. "Gary, his younger son, doesn't have the same blood type
as either one of his parents. Doug is B-positive and Patti is B-negative
and Gary is type A."

"That's right," Doug agreed, as if this loaded piece of information
had simply slipped his mind. "When Gary had his school physical—
he couldn't have been more than seven or eight—I asked him what his
blood type was, and he told me."

"Did he ever realize that you weren't his real—I mean, biological—
father?"

Doug shook his head. "He didn't; I never told him."

"And did that knowledge alter your relationship with him?"
I asked.

He shook his head again. "Not at all. But with Patti, it did. Not that I hadn't already realized that things were very, very wrong between us." I was puzzled by the absence of any affect in his expression and his voice. Then he added that, oddly enough, his older son had a high-strung personality very like that of his ex-wife, while his second son (unrelated to him by blood) had a personality far more similar to his own.

"Would you describe yourself as an easygoing person?" I asked him.

"Oh yes," Claudia said warmly, before her husband could respond. "He really is the most laid-back, easygoing human being."

AN ABUSE OF AUTHORITY?

I asked Claudia what had been happening in her own life during the ten or more years between the end of her first marriage and her meeting and marrying Doug. She told me that she had gone back to school to earn her bachelor's degree and then continued on to get a master's degree in psychology.

"My specializations were in psychometric assessment and school psychology. When I met Doug, I was a psychiatric social worker. At the time, I'd been dating various people, but nothing special was happening." Her voice held a peculiarly doubtful note, and I saw her glance at her husband as if requesting his permission to continue. If he responded, I didn't see it happen.

"And during that whole decade or so, was there any significant relationship in your life?" I inquired.

"Yes," Claudia responded quietly, looking down at her hands, which were folded on her lap.

I fixed my gaze on her, as if urging her to continue, and she said, "I was dating a Catholic priest for most of that period. I think I'd stopped seeing him about a year before I met Douglas." I glanced at Doug, whose impassive face betrayed no sign of consternation. He'd clearly heard this whole story before.

Claudia's affair with the clergyman had begun during the time she'd been newly separated from her first husband. "It started as Father—I mean, Paul, the priest—was counseling me," Claudia said.

During that psychologically fragile period of her life, her relationship with the cleric had slowly changed from a deeply caring friendship into a sexual affair. This secret relationship lasted for several years, and nobody who knew them (including her parents) ever suspected anything.

"I don't know what my mother and father were *thinking!*" Claudia shook her head from side to side, then laughed incredulously. "I mean, Paul and I would go off for a weekend, and my folks were so proud—I was Father Paul's special friend. The idea that anything *sexual* might be going on never seemed to enter their minds!"

I was silent for a moment, for I was reflecting on the spate of recent articles about inappropriate relations between Catholic clergy and their parishioners. "I know you were an adult at the time, but now, looking back on that affair, do you think of Paul's behavior as an abuse of priestly authority?" I asked her, keeping my voice carefully neutral.

Claudia nodded, her expression taut. "*Now* I do. Now I look upon it as an abuse of power."

We were quiet for a few moments. Then I asked her how and why that relationship came to an end. "Was there a real breakup or did it eventually morph back into a friendship?"

"I wanted *more,*" Claudia said tersely, her words clipped. "I wanted him to leave the Church and marry me. And at that point, he said he just couldn't."

"So you knew he was already married—married to his vocation?" It was a statement in the form of a question, and she nodded. "Yes," she said, looking aggrieved by the memory.

I paused, my thoughts drifting back to Claudia's starring role in her original family's drama. She had been the delightful apple of her father's eye throughout her childhood, even as her mother was being neglected and slighted. So this priest-lover had been the second supportive, caring "Father" who had selected her to be his (inappropriate) special person. Claudia had spent more than the first three decades of her life being courted by the Impossible Man, when it came to forging a feasible adult relationship.

"MY BRAIN WAS OUT TO LUNCH"

My interview with the Hamiltons proceeded with the usual questions about whether and how much they had projected their thoughts forward into the future. Given the extension of the human life span, and the fact that they were both in their early sixties, many years of relatively active living could await them. Had they made plans about their eventual retirement, and pictured ways in which they would want to spend their days when neither of them was any longer in the work world?

Doug said glumly that he was already retired; he had been forced out of his job fourteen years earlier. This had happened in the wake of a serious accident at a time when he'd been employed as a skilled machinist at a company that manufactured airplane parts. "I was working on a machine, and it came apart and beat me half to death.

The only thing that saved my life was that I put my hands up to
my face."

"He's been diagnosed as having had a traumatic brain injury,"
Claudia said evenly.

I asked her how long they'd been married at the time of the accident. "Let's see, we were married in 1981, and he had the accident in
1988. Seven years. It wasn't a long time," she replied wistfully, glancing at her husband with the mixture of concern and caring one might
see on the face of a worried mother.

Doug laughed a short, wry laugh. "The funny thing is that it happened just six days after I'd gotten a safety award. A five-year award
for a record of perfect safety on the job." His wife placed a light, sympathetic hand on his shoulder, and let it rest there.

I looked at her hand, and then at the tender expression on her face.
"You are devoted to him, Claudia, aren't you?" I asked.

"Yes, I am," she answered without hesitation. But then she paused,
added that in all honesty the marriage had reached a very rocky point
in the period following the accident.

"That was because she didn't understand what had happened to my
body," Doug said. "I looked normal, but I wasn't."

The freak mishap had left him with a wide assortment of cerebral
symptoms ranging from a short attention span to migraines to memory
problems to a disturbing, constant ringing in his ears to difficulties
with impulse control. In fact, his job as a machinist had been termi-
nated after an incident in which he'd lost his temper and thrown a
hammer at his foreman.

I gazed at Doug Hamilton a few moments, thinking that this didn't
sound anything like the easygoing person he'd described himself as
being. Doug met my gaze and, to my surprise, replied to my unvoiced

question. "I *looked* normal," he repeated, "but my brain was out to lunch."

He explained that he'd been taking several kinds of medications post-injury, but those medicines hadn't helped. "I told my doctors, 'This isn't working,' but they weren't listening. I mean, my whole body had kicked out of gear. Finally, I got their attention, but it took a while to get them to listen to me . . . and that caused problems," he explained.

The Hamiltons had owned a house at that time—one bought with the settlement proceeds from Doug's accident—and Claudia felt that managing it was more than she could handle. "He just wouldn't do anything to keep the place going. He wouldn't mow the lawn or rake the leaves—and we were in financial difficulties then. Money was extremely tight. I was working and going to graduate school. My newly widowed mother was living with us, too. . . . And I guess that after a while, I started thinking that maybe Doug was just faking it."

"I can sum up what was happening: I was out of control, and I couldn't do anything about it," he said contritely.

The couple's arguments about money, tasks and the upkeep of their home eventually reached a point where Claudia felt she had two options: she could either put their house on the market, or see the marriage fall apart. So the Hamiltons sold their home for a good price, one that left them with a comfortable nest egg. They rented a condo on the Connecticut shoreline and later—when they were in their mid-fifties—purchased a condo in Florida, where they planned to retire eventually.

"Selling that house was definitely the smartest thing we ever did," Claudia stated. "Because, one, it got us off the financial hook, and, two, we got rid of the thing we were constantly fighting about."

The Weight of the World

Still, when I reached the following questions—How about income and finances? How is money managed, and how are financial decisions made? Does money tend to be a source of tension?—I heard an audible intake of breath.

The Hamiltons turned to each other making faces of mock horror, and then they both burst out laughing. I laughed, too, but said I didn't think I had said anything funny.

Claudia, still laughing, assured me wryly that if they *were* fighting, money was the thing they were fighting about! Then she said that they had a "fifty-dollar rule."

"Doug is not allowed to spend more than fifty dollars at a time without consulting me. He doesn't have a lot of impulse control, in general, especially when it comes to Home Shopping Network or QVC. That's only been since his accident. Other than that rule, we never move money from one account to another without discussing it, and most financial decisions are made jointly. Still, money is probably the only thing we ever fight about."

"And what would a typical fight be like? What would start it?" I asked.

"No money," Claudia said, and Doug said, "No money," in almost the same breath.

If they ran out of Claudia's salary before the end of the month, it meant taking funds out of their joint savings account. "I have a tendency to get really upset if we have to do that," she said. "For instance, if there is a bill coming from the Florida condominium that I hadn't anticipated, I feel overwhelmed."

She told me then that a recent hurricane in Florida had cost them a devastating $10,000 in repair bills. For this couple, an unexpected debt of that magnitude would have been the financial equivalent of a serious automobile accident for which they were uninsured.

"The weight of the world is on your shoulders," I said to Claudia quietly, and she nodded, said that was how it felt to her.

"So when you're feeling strained about the money situation," I ventured carefully, "is that a time when you're liable to start a quarrel with Doug?" I posed the question in that way because I remembered from our long-ago interviews that Claudia DeNatale had been prone to sudden outbursts of rage when she was under too much pressure and found it hard to cope.

She met my gaze swiftly and said, a guilty half-smile on her face, "Yes, and what we'll end up fighting about is usually something that has nothing to do with money. But it's tension about money that sparks it, really."

I turned to Doug and asked him how he felt about that.

He shrugged and said stoutly, "Sometimes it bothers me, sometimes it doesn't. It just happens. But why should I get upset if there's nothing I can do about it? Why should I scream and holler if it's nothing I can control?"

I asked Claudia if he ever *did* scream and holler. She shook her head no.

"So *you* just scream and holler?" I asked her.

"Yes," she said. I didn't reply, but my own thought was that a quarrel with someone who wasn't responding would be one I'd find extremely frustrating.

"What I do is, I *listen*," Doug stated evenly.

"You just sit there and listen?" I asked.

"Yes," he replied, adding that he had raised his voice to his wife perhaps one or two times in the twenty-five years they'd been married. He just heard her out, and along the way tried to interject useful suggestions.

"It's true," Claudia said, with a nod of agreement. Then she added with a self-deprecating shrug, "But as you know, I've never won any awards for my lack of temper." Her cheeks had reddened. "And I have to say that Doug will often come up with some very logical suggestions. It's just that logic is really not what I'm looking for at that moment." As she said these words I thought I saw an expression of fear flicker across her features.

"You're dealing with terror," I observed flatly.

"Yes," Claudia said soberly.

"Yes," Doug agreed, "And she shouldn't be. She should be worrying about herself. That's why I don't say anything."

I kept my gaze on Claudia. "You're feeling the burdens," I said, and she nodded. "Because they're resting on you," I added.

"Yes," she said again.

"Not only that, but I get a sense of your worry about Doug. It feels"—I hesitated—"it feels quite . . . maternal to me."

Claudia's eyes widened, as if my remark had surprised her. "Someone in my women's group *said* that to me!" she responded. A moment later she added gently, "I do feel quite maternal about Doug."

MORE BAD NEWS

The Florida repair bill was not the only financial setback the Hamiltons had been forced to absorb. "Up until recently, I was counting off the days until I could retire," Claudia said. "I fully expected to do so when I reached age sixty-three. And now I've found out that I'm not going to be able to do that until at least sixty-five. This news actually came as a big shock to me."

I asked her what had happened.

"Well, I expected to be able to arrange to pay back dues in the teachers' union—for years that I worked when the union didn't recognize adult education—and, in exchange, receive a higher pension from the teachers' retirement plan. But I've just been given official notice that I'm not going to be able to do that. It was something about my licensing that makes me ineligible to do so." Claudia gave a small, helpless shake of her head as if she were at a loss to understand why this adverse bureaucratic judgment had come down.

She said that in the wake of that setback, she'd felt demoralized and depressed. Nevertheless she had bounced back fairly quickly. Claudia said, "I began to realize that if I *did* retire, I really wouldn't know what to do with myself. So much of my life is invested in my job—so much of my identity—that if I didn't have it, I'm not sure what I would do."

I smiled. "You don't want to learn pottery or become a painter? There's not something that you're just dying to do but can't do because you are working?"

Claudia laughed and shook her head no.

I was silent for a few moments, because I myself was feeling nonplussed by this bureaucratic delay of Claudia's well-deserved pension. She had been administering and teaching in a state-run adult education program for many years, and at present held a senior position. She taught math skills, English as a second language and high school completion, and her workday was a long one.

Most of Claudia Hamilton's students were immigrants, and she truly enjoyed working with them and getting to know them. But the job also involved long commutes, for she taught at sites in two different cities, and they were both more than an hour's drive from her home.

"I leave my house at eight o'clock in the morning, and most days I don't get back until seven-thirty or eight at night," she said, adding that she found the commuting more exhausting than anything else. "It's hard on my back, and the hours of traveling are just grueling." I winced, because long auto trips are hard on my own back, too.

"How about energy? Do you have enough energy for the job?"

Her face clouded over. "No, I don't; not as much as I used to. And I think that's where the ambivalence comes in. I'm beginning to find my job very, very tiring."

"There's the mental strain, too," Doug said.

"It's just mushrooming," Claudia acknowledged.

But it was clear that the couple's retirement was out of the question for the foreseeable future. They didn't have the resources to support it.

A CATCH-22

The company Doug Hamilton had worked for had given him a cash settlement after his accident, but had also managed to cut his pension in half due to a so-called break in service—the time he'd been away serving in the military. "The state let them get away with that," Doug said. "Connecticut is not a workman-friendly state—at least, not to workers who get hurt."

Doug was now on Social Security disability, plus his small company pension. Clearly, the couple's economic survival was dependent on Claudia's continuing to work until her own pension came through. I asked the Hamiltons whether they were giving any consideration to putting their Florida condo up for sale.

"That's a dilemma right now," Claudia said, and Doug added, "The tax bite is awfully big if we give it up. It's over twenty percent of any profit we might make. At the same time, it's costing us an awful lot of money to keep it."

"Per year," his wife said emphatically. "And all the money that I'm spending to keep the place down there is money that I could be putting away toward retirement. Right now, we have almost no retirement money."

Doug then told me that if one of them could live in Florida permanently, most of the condo payments would shrink considerably. "The taxes would be down to nothing, because of the Homestead Act. Without the Homestead Act, they're very high. They raised the assessment on our place ten times already—it's overinflated."

As Claudia explained, the homestead tax exemption is a state law that permits the owner of a home, condo, co-op or mobile home who *occupies the residence on a continuous basis* to subtract the first $25,000 from the assessed value of his or her property. "We would be paying twelve hundred or thirteen hundred in taxes versus the five thousand we're paying now," she said. "But instead, the upkeep of the Florida place is costing me—costing us—about ten thousand a year. So what's happening is that I'm having trouble saving any part of my salary for retirement."

"It's getting eaten away by Florida," Doug said glumly.

Moreover, the rules of the condo community strictly forbade rentals, so the Hamiltons could not use the condo to generate income in that way. "It's really a catch-22, because if I were to retire to Florida now, we wouldn't have enough money to live on," Claudia said. "But if we let go of the place, we'd never be able to get anything like it at near the same price. So I don't know what to do. I really don't." She looked at me appealingly, as if I might somehow provide the magical answer.

I wished I could, but I couldn't. "Well," I said, raising both hands in a gesture of helplessness, "it sounds as if you got yourself involved in another piece of real estate."

Claudia nodded, laughed ruefully. "Absolutely! I said that to Doug just a couple of weeks ago. We did it to ourselves again! We shouldn't own anything. The minute we own any kind of property, we start not getting along . . . really."

To which Doug added that in any case, the condo would be hard to sell now because there were so many places still empty due to the terrible hurricane their Florida community had experienced two years earlier.

FINANCIAL GERONTOLOGY

The good news—the remarkable news—is that on average, people are living years longer than could have been imagined at the outset of the twentieth century. But, from a financial point of view, the worrying news is that the assets they have accumulated during their highest earning years may not be sufficient to sustain them through the elongated life cycle.

At present, we live in an aging population—one in which a baby boomer will be reaching age sixty every seven seconds for the next two decades. Moreover, two out of every five Americans are now acting as caregivers for elderly relatives. This may be happening even as they themselves are figuring out when and how they will leave the workforce and spend their own retirement years.

An interesting, relatively recent development has been a field of

study called financial gerontology, or "the science of wealth span planning," pioneered by Professor Neal Cutler, a founding father of the
American Institute of Financial Gerontology (AIFG). As Dr. Cutler
explained to me during a series of conversations, the early years of
adult life are devoted to the key goal of accumulating assets, and
doing so in a methodical way that will reduce the risk of penalties and
losses. This generally means developing a diversified portfolio—
investing one's savings in an assortment of bonds, mutual funds, stocks
and so forth.

In the earlier part of the twentieth century, Cutler said, the important thing was for the wage earner in his earlier adult years to link up
with an expert in financial markets and investments. But today, with
all the online information and the how-to investment books available, people are much more sophisticated when they seek a financial
planner to help them plan a robust portfolio. Said Cutler, who is also
acting director of the Gerontology Center of the University of North
Carolina: "They are looking for a highly skilled professional who can
collaborate with them in using this knowledge to the maximum
advantage."

During the accumulation phase of adulthood (the twenties, thirties,
forties, plus), the individual is usually growing his or her family—and
therefore spending money on refrigerators, clothing, cars, school fees
and so forth—but the primary function of these early decades is to
amass enough wealth to last throughout the second (or "distribution")
stage of the life span. Thus, it is vital to figure out how best to invest,
diversify and protect one's growing nest egg during the early adult
years when earning power is reaching its eventual maximum.

At some point in the wealth span cycle, however, one must begin
looking forward to the second stage—the "distribution" or expendi-

ture part of the life course. During this phase a person may not be completely retired (many baby boomers choose to continue working part-time) but he or she will not be earning at the same rate as during the top-compensation years when he commanded his full salary.

In the expenditure stage of the wealth span/life span, when an individual is looking forward to an eventual full retirement (and perhaps even much earlier, if the person is caring for an aging parent), it can be extremely helpful to be in touch with a professional who is well informed about the aging process. A financial planner with a gerontological background is often capable of giving advice on the distribution phase that even the canniest accumulation-phase planner may not know about.

In Neal Cutler's view, a professional financial planner should be expert in the art of accumulating wealth—that is, investing and protecting the client's assets. "And most of them *are*, because for years and years, when the boomers were young, the largest chunk of the market consisted of people who were in that accumulation stage," he said.

Now, though, financial planners are realizing that their once-forty-year-old clients are moving into their sixties. And the major task is moving from pure accumulation issues to those relating to the expenditure stage. "The planners now need to add on some additional nuts and bolts—the gerontological expertise—such as the rules about withdrawing money from an IRA at the right times, so you don't take out too much or too little. Also, making sure your beneficiaries are lined up in the correct way—because sometimes the age of the beneficiary has an impact on how much you must take out of an IRA. There are a host of technical issues of this kind, including a fine-tuned understanding of Medicare, Medicaid and long-term health care planning, " Cutler observed.

The only "students" who are qualified to matriculate at the American Institute of Financial Gerontology are those who are already professional financial planners. Once admitted to the AIFG, these students attend a series of weekend courses and seminars where they are instructed in the biology, psychology, sociology and demography of aging. They learn not only about the aging process itself but about issues of individual aging and issues of family aging as well. The challenges of family aging can, as we all know, be matters of great passion, anger and misunderstanding as the needs of one or more family members come into conflict with those of others.

In brief, Cutler said, the AIFG's goal is to produce the kind of financial counselor who has both technical "accumulation" *and* "expenditure" expertise, plus a profound understanding of gerontology.

THE FLORIDA CONDO

In terms of wealth, the Hamiltons' life savings was $40,000. They kept this in a tax-sheltered account that yielded 6½ percent yearly interest. Given that they were both just moving into their early sixties, the "expenditure" side of their equation seemed woefully insufficient. As our discussion moved along, I asked Doug if he had thought about how he would get along if Claudia were to die before he did.

"I *don't* think about it," he replied. "Why worry about something that is going to happen when you don't know *when* it's going to happen?"

Claudia smiled, said he was like the proverbial ostrich with his head in the sand.

"What can you do, I'm asking? What can you do?" Doug protested. "If she died right now, what could I do?"

I hesitated, then said that perhaps the only thing he could do was to give some thought to what life would be like for him if he were to find himself on his own. His facial expression remained composed, but he said that for a while it would probably be very lonely.

"That's what it would be like, very lonely," he repeated. "But I would live. I would live and go on." A note in his voice suggested he had nothing more to say on this subject.

I turned to Claudia. "What would it be like for you?"

"I worry all the time about what will happen to *him*," she said. "I would be fine."

I smiled. "So Doug doesn't have to do the worrying. You—"

She laughed good-naturedly and completed my thought. "Yes, I worry for the two of us. Douglas is not a worrier; he doesn't have to be. Because I'm so very good at it!"

"That's a DeNatale family trait," observed her husband, as if on the emotional sidelines.

"He would be totally taken care of. I've made arrangements with my sister Gemma, and she would pay his bills. When I retire, I will set up my retirement fund so that in the event of my death, the stipend would go to him. I've set up my insurance policies, too, so that he is the beneficiary, and Gemma would hold the money in trust for him. So he doesn't need to worry. And as for me, financially speaking, I would be able to go on. Because I bring in more money than he does."

She paused, then said in a troubled tone of voice, "Still, I do worry tremendously about him."

I smiled and suggested that she worry about herself for a moment. "What would it be like for you if you found yourself on your own?"

Claudia frowned. "I would be lonely . . . for a while."

"Where would you think of living if you were on your own?"

"*Not* Florida," she stated without hesitation.

I was taken aback. The Florida condo had taken a hefty bite out of their very limited savings. "No?" I said. "So that place is only for vacations? You said you were keeping it for retirement."

"For the two of us," Doug put in firmly. "I wish you could see it," he added, a dreamy expression crossing his usually impassive face. "The place is beautiful."

It didn't make sense to me. "For the two of you, but then *you*, Claudia, would zip right back up north if you were on your own?" I asked her.

She nodded and said with no uncertainty, "I would zip back to the East Coast in a minute."

"To be nearer to your sister and your nephews?"

She nodded again, said yes, to be nearer to her sister and her cousins—friends, too. "Some of them are childhood friends. Actually, one of them I've known since I was three years old. So they are lifetime friends of mine." I was mystified. Her major network of support—which gerontologists consider to be increasingly crucial to health and well-being as we age—was all located in the area in which the Hamiltons were now living.

So why, from a financial point of view, had Claudia invested so heavily in the move to Florida? And why was she even contemplating moving there after her retirement?

THE GOLDEN DREAM

I was quiet for a few moments, sat there tapping my pencil on the sketch pad on my lap. I had to step back from this discussion and think about a question: *Why* were they moving to Florida? Why were they clinging to this idea if it was so far from Claudia's best choice and was also one that might put Doug in some peril?

For, if he were left to his own devices, who would enforce the "fifty-dollar rule" on impulsive spending? Furthermore, with Claudia's sister Gemma living far away, how could she oversee his budget and his expenditures? Doug wouldn't be able to handle these matters easily without a caring person's assistance.

So why were they going to Florida at all? My own suspicion was that it had to do with some idealized picture of retirement, one in which Florida was the dream location where they could spend their blissful later years together. They had bought the condo eleven years ago, when they were in their early fifties; however, it seemed to me that over time the upside of the plan was receding.

It was clear that retiring in Florida had been a joint project. Neither spouse had said, "I'm going to Florida myself"; but now the notion of the shared marital idyll appeared to be diminishing. What *did* remain was their willingness to hang on to this plan for dear life—so that despite the bad luck they'd encountered, their financial shakiness and Doug's health challenges, they could still cling to the happy vision that hovered in the distance.

Meanwhile the downside of the dream was becoming ever more apparent. Claudia's statement about being uprooted from her child-hood friends and her relatives suggested that for her, the idealized picture hatched in the couple's mid-fifties was unraveling as they moved ever closer to it. They would be retreating from a familiar setting to an unaccustomed one. It would be a world filled with strangers, a world in which they would have to find new doctors, a chiropractor (for Claudia's back), a dry cleaner, a pharmacy and so forth. They would also have to develop a whole new circle of friends—which isn't always easy. Furthermore, given Doug's health challenges, these new friends would have to be people who were especially supportive and understanding.

I thought about Claudia's remark—"We should never own real estate"—and her ironic laugh when she said it. Why, then, were they persisting with this plan? A move to Florida would, in and of itself, be a major life event—and a cost they could ill afford. Why did this whole project continue to make sense to them? There was a pattern here of holding on to something—the dream of the golden land that the pair had been holding on to for the past eleven years. At the moment, even though the glow was fading a bit—Claudia was obviously doing some second-guessing—the Hamiltons were still vectored toward a move I feared might be detrimental to one or both of them.

FACTS AND FIGURES

Let me digress from the interview itself to reflect on the Hamiltons' shaky finances and the dilemma they were dealing with at the moment. This was, in abbreviated form, *If we move to the Florida condo now, we can't afford to live. If we stay up north, the condo will prevent us from amassing any savings.* In truth, the condo did seem like a money pit into which their resources were steadily disappearing.

The pair's financial situation at the moment was as follows: Doug brought in $1,200 in Social Security disability payments and $381 from his pension, for a total of $1,581 per month. Claudia's take-home salary was $6,250 per month (an overall figure that included her ten-month contract and the summer months during which she taught and administered her adult ed program as well).

If she retired at age sixty-five, which she planned to do, she would earn $1,100 a month in Social Security payments and $500 per month from her pension. This would mean a dramatic drop in her income, more than $4,600 per month. This, combined with Doug's monthly income, didn't amount to a handsome amount to live on. As for the $40,000 in savings, this was all the money that remained of the larger settlement that Doug had received from his former employers.

Where did the luxury of a Florida condo, sitting empty except for Claudia's few weeks of vacation time per year, fit into this kind of financial picture? I put this question to several authorities in the fields of retirement and gerontology.

One expert reacted by focusing on the fact that the Hamiltons' Florida plan had been made years earlier, when they were in their early fifties. Now, as the reality of retirement loomed ever closer, one partner (Doug) still seemed as strongly invested in it as ever. The other partner (Claudia) seemed, however, to be experiencing an increasing number of reservations. For her, a permanent relocation to the condo would involve leaving the support system of a lifetime behind her.

"Given their limited resources," this retirement counselor commented, "I wonder why the couple is persisting with this project. Wouldn't it be wiser to take stock and reevaluate it at this much later point in time? How does it seem to make sense to them?"

Good questions, I thought, for in many respects the Hamiltons' Florida plan didn't make a great deal of sense to me, either.

Another expert in the field pointed out that the social services in Florida are far inferior to those available in Connecticut. "Thirty years ago the whole idea being promoted was 'Come down to Florida, all you wealthy, healthy older people. Come and enjoy the weather and play tennis and swim.' " But now, this gerontologist said, those hale and hardy adults have aged, and the social services have not kept pace; these services are seriously underdeveloped and shorthanded. "When you balance it out—excepting, of course, for the weather—Connecticut is a far wiser state in which to grow old."

Why not, he asked, sell the Florida condo as quickly as possible and invest the proceeds in some interest-earning financial mechanism? The reasoning of this highly knowledgeable professional was very much in line with my own.

Subsequently, however, a conversation with financial professional Cathy Daignault—who has extensive experience in dealing with issues relating to retirement—had the effect of turning my opinions on their axis. I began to see the Hamiltons' situation from a different and somewhat more complex perspective.

I met with Ms. Daignault in her firm's North Haven, Connecticut, office. Interestingly enough, Daignault was the first female financial counselor I consulted, and she was the first person to focus on the real-life emotional aspects of the situation. It was clearly this husband's heart's desire to retire in Florida, and his wife had once supported the plan—so much so that she had agreed to the condo's purchase in the first place. "It's his dream," Daignault said thoughtfully, "but in a way, she seems to be locked into it."

It wasn't difficult to understand why. Doug Hamilton had suffered such severe blows in his lifetime—the flagrantly unfaithful first wife; the disabling, life-changing accident—that it would be hard to deliver him yet another severe disappointment.

While she would never, Daignault told me, have counseled a couple in their situation to make the purchase in the first place, the reality was that they *were* now the condo's owners. And there were in fact certain pluses to the situation in which they found themselves, she added, as she surveyed the financial data I'd supplied to her. For one thing, the couple was now paying rent in Connecticut—$762 a month, which was roughly $9,000 per year. Therefore, the counselor said, if they could hang on to their condo until Claudia's retirement, that expense would go away, for then they would be living in a place that they *owned*. And even though, in the interim, they would be supporting two different residences, the money going to the condo wasn't being totally lost. "They are paying down the principal on their mortgage and getting a deduction on their federal tax return. So even if the Florida condo was costing them as much as twelve thousand a year, it would only be nine thousand in reality," Daignault pointed out.

Furthermore, she said, if the couple did go down to Florida and lived in their condo for two consecutive years, they would be considered bona fide residents of that state. As such, if they then chose to turn around and sell their place, they would avoid paying federal and state taxes on the sale. I knew that the Hamiltons had bought their condo for a very good price—$68,000—and its value had climbed in the intervening eleven years. Claudia thought that its worth was now in the neighborhood of $120,000.

As we went over the basic facts and figures of the Hamiltons' circumstances, Daignault had some other important nuggets of information to offer. She explained that if Claudia Hamilton worked for one extra year—that is, until she reached age sixty-six years and zero months—she would receive her full Social Security entitlement. This would amount to $785 more per month than if she took it right now. "That sum is, of course, subject to inflation, so it goes up every year," she said. It might well be even more by the time that Claudia retired.

But in the event that Claudia were to die first and her sister became Doug's trustee, what would happen? Wouldn't the distance between Connecticut and Florida be a dangerously faraway one for him?

Cathy Daignault shook her head and said that if at some future date his sister-in-law became his trustee, administering Doug's estate from afar was perfectly feasible. "I myself handle my mother's affairs, and she is in an assisted-living facility in Florida. All that means," Daignault explained with a friendly smile, "is that her bills are sent to me and I pay them."

I smiled, too, but nevertheless wondered about the Hamiltons' fifty-dollar rule. If Claudia was no longer with him, who would be there to limit Doug's impulse buying?

A TIME OF RENEWAL OR A TIME OF DISTANCE?

I knew, from many prior interviews, that to the question *What role do faith and religion play in your life?* I would usually receive a variant on a basic answer. Whether the respondent was a believer or not, a frequent churchgoer or temple-goer or not, the person would always describe him- or herself as a "deeply spiritual human being."

When I asked this question of the Hamiltons, I learned that Doug had left the Baptist Church for the Catholic Church and remained a Catholic even though Claudia had recently dropped out. Doug wasn't attending services regularly at the moment, but he was looking around for a church that "felt right" to him.

"I miss it," he said, "because we used to go all the time. Something happened when her kid sister died. . . . Right now, she's not too interested in the Church." The Hamiltons had told me of Claudia's younger sister's death from liver cancer a year earlier.

"What did happen, Claudia?" I asked, but Doug answered for her. "She's mad at the world right now. She has to . . . I don't know . . . She has to let life pass by for a little bit. Then she'll be all right," he said amiably.

"Is that how you would answer the question?" I asked Claudia.

She shook her head no. "I've had trouble with the Catholic Church ever since that affair. And now, with all this stuff coming out in the papers, I don't believe . . ." Her voice trailed off.

We were silent for a moment, and then she said, "I think I'm more spiritual than I am religious. I think that we all have inside of us a core of goodness and a spiritual side that makes us want to do good things for people. And I think that what counts is how we act, and what we do. It's not showing up in church once a week and honoring something that may or may not exist. Mostly, I don't think it exists. My kid sister Angie's philosophy was that people, when they die, don't obviously go to some place called 'heaven' or some place called 'hell.' She believed that matter can't be created and it can't be destroyed—it can only change form, and that therefore it will always be present in the stars, the sun, the grass. . . ." Her voice trailed off again.

"That sounds somewhat like a Hindu belief," I said.

Claudia nodded her agreement, said with conviction in her voice, "I suppose I've adopted that philosophy myself."

"Is this a time of increased understanding and renewal, or is there a sense of making a peace in place and having increased distance?" was the next question I posed to the Hamiltons (a pro forma query, because I knew the answer already).

Claudia was the first to respond. "The first part, yes. I think we have a far better understanding of each other. I would say this is a really good time in our marriage."

Doug said, "I would say the same, that we understand each other much better."

"And you would both use the word 'renewal' in the same way?" They nodded in unison.

"I would actually say this is the happiest period of my whole life-time," Claudia said.

I was surprised, given the financial and other worries that con-fronted the pair. "Why is that?" I asked her.

"Because I'm living with someone who loves me unconditionally," she said simply. "Doug does love me that way, and that has never been part of my experience, not with anyone." She took in a deep breath and then exhaled, saying, "I include my parents. Oh yes, I was my father's darling pet, but everything had to happen on *his* terms."

A note of bitterness had crept into her voice as she spoke. She turned to her husband and met his gaze fully, as if seeking the sympa-thy and reassurance to be found there.

"What do you think are the major sexual issues that emerge at this time of life?" was the next question on my list. Doug laughed shortly. "Medication," was his one-word answer.

Claudia explained that Doug was on a cocktail of powerful drugs, including antidepressants and antiseizure medicines. These affected his sex drive. But she, too, was on antidepressants from time to time, when exhaustion and concerns about their finances were getting her down.

"It's really *my* medications," Doug insisted, intent on shouldering the blame.

"So where sex is concerned, you've just quit?" I asked them, looking from one to the other. They both nodded. I was silent momentarily, recalling a just-published study of the sexual lives of 3,005 older adults that had appeared in the *New England Journal of Medicine*. There, it was reported that more than one-quarter (27 percent) of peo-ple in their age group had not had sex with a partner in the course of the previous year.

"Does it bother either one of you?" I asked, looking from Claudia to Doug.

"It bothers *me*," he said. "I don't know why, but it does. Immensely."

"Does it bother you because of urges? Or does it bother you because it's just not right?" I asked him.

He shrugged. "Both," he said.

I turned to Claudia. "How about you?"

"It doesn't bother me at all," she said.

"It doesn't bother you at all?" I asked again, and she raised her shoulders briefly as if to say, "Everything is fine."

I asked Doug whether he had ever tried any of the new drugs— such as Viagra—for his missing "urges."

Claudia said that his doctor had put him on Cialis, but it hadn't helped.

"You have to have the urge to have it work, so it really doesn't make much difference," Doug explained to me carefully. "I may have the urge sometimes, but it's not necessarily when I take the medication. You have to have the urge and the medication at the same time, you see. It's like blowing up a balloon: if you don't have any air, you can't blow the balloon up."

I thought of Claudia's schedule, and the long hours she was away from home. "Are you saying that sometimes you have the urge but Claudia is not around; and that when she is around you might not have taken the medication?" I asked.

"Exactly," Doug said.

"And in any case, Claudia isn't that interested, right?"

It was Claudia herself who responded to this question. "I think that's probably it," she said quietly.

I looked at her for a long moment, and then I looked at Doug.

"Then what you're telling me is that it's a tender, loving relationship, but it's not a tender, loving, sexual relationship?

"Yes, but it's still great; trust me," Doug said, and then the Hamiltons exchanged one of those long, fixed gazes that psychologists have termed "eye love"—the protracted gaze exchanged by a mother and her baby, or by two people who are falling in love.

Chapter Nine

NANCY AND DAVID STERNBERG

IN SICKNESS AND IN HEALTH

A s I drove into the wide semicircular driveway of the Sternbergs' sprawling ranch-style home in Westport, Connecticut, I had the eerie feeling of having arrived in a time capsule. True, the laurel bushes around the house had grown thicker and taller, but everything else about the place was just as I remembered it. It had been some twenty years since I had visited with Nancy and David Sternberg, which had been at the time of our intensive interviews for my first book on couples, *Intimate Partners*. The Sternbergs were in their late forties at the time—the oldest couple in that book—and right now, David's seventieth birthday was approaching.

They both came out to greet me as I unloaded my recording gear from the car. They were all smiles and seemed pleased at the prospect of another round of interviews. Clearly, these past years had treated them kindly. David, who is over six feet tall, looked slender and fit. He had a slightly receding hairline, but an abundance of soft, dark hair that was slowly graying at the temples. Nancy, who is on the order of five and a half feet tall, now wore her blond hair in a short, attractive bob with lighter highlights that gleamed in a bright Indian summer sunshine. The Sternbergs were both dressed in gym gear and told me they'd just returned from their daily morning workout.

As they ushered me inside, I took note of how well—even relaxed—both of them looked. I well remembered our discussions of the stormy early years of this couple's marriage, for I'd talked with them at prodigious length these many years earlier. I knew that throughout the initial decades of their life together they had fought about anything and everything married partners can fight about—money, the upkeep of the house, disciplining their young children—and a variety of other issues that revolved around the question of: Who is the person in control? Nancy Sternberg may have looked slender and petite next to her long, lanky husband, but I was well aware that she was capable of holding her ground against what had been her spouse's sometimes intimidating, demanding, even irrational behavior.

Before I met them, the Sternbergs had worked hard—in two years of intensive couples' therapy—to free themselves from the spell of their own pasts in their families of origin. David was the angry son of a domineering, competitive parent—a father who'd attempted to rule those around him with his money and his disapproval. David had spent the early years of his adulthood in a frantic effort to show his father up. He wanted to demonstrate that he was well able to make his own way in the world, and that he didn't need anything from his ferociously critical parent. "For my father, money was love. Money was control," David said, on many occasions. He had had far less to say about his mother, who had been a shadowy presence and seriously depressed throughout much of his childhood.

Depression seemed to run in David's family, for his sister suffered from the disorder and had committed suicide in her late thirties. David also suffered periodic depressions and had made some half-hearted suicide attempts himself during the course of the marriage. When he'd first met Nancy Fine, his wife-to-be, David had recognized that she was not only a beautiful woman, she was someone with a kind heart who was a natural caretaker.

"I come from a long line of caretakers," Nancy had told me during those earlier interviews. "My mother was a caretaker, my grandmother was a caretaker and I am one, too." Nancy recounted David's method of courtship—it had been "like a tornado"—and she'd been over-whelmed by this young man who was highly intelligent, urbane and yet endearingly needful. The couple were in their early twenties when they wed and began raising a family.

But the marital pact that the Sternbergs were entering had not been clearly spelled out. David assumed that he was in command and would give all the orders, and Nancy would follow them accordingly. This was the way it had been in his own family: his father handed down the orders and his mother had always obeyed them without question.

As a result, David would say things to his wife such as "Today I think it would be appropriate for you to vacuum and clean the bathrooms." Nancy, in recounting this behavior to me, had imitated his stentorian tone of voice.

"What was I, the paid slave?" She laughed, shook her head, then said indignantly, "He had the wrong person." During that period, David was a man in a frenzy, working three demanding jobs simultaneously and absent from his children's lives most of the time. He was engaged in a feverish effort to show his antagonistic father that he was not only equally capable as a man but also smarter and *better* at earning a substantial living. And in truth, David was prospering, but the net effect of his driven behavior was that he'd landed in the hospital after a heart attack at the age of thirty-three.

As bad luck would have it, this occurred at a time when Nancy was mourning the loss of her beloved mother, who had died from breast cancer a few months earlier. The Sternbergs' difficulties—and their constant misunderstandings and quarrels—intensified even further during the months of David's slow recovery and a subsequent serious depression. Nancy was holding down a part-time job in a nearby pharmaceutical laboratory, running the family, caring for her burdensome husband and keeping his business ventures afloat simultaneously. The couple's difficulties further intensified when their oldest son, Greg, age ten, began "exploding"—showing symptoms of disturbed behavior both in school and with friends.

Nevertheless, despite all the ongoing friction, illness and family problems, Nancy and David had remained emotionally and sexually bonded to each other. In some fundamental way, the Sternbergs did love each other—both said so, without uncertainty in their voices, numerous times throughout the course of our interviews. Nancy did, however, recall a certain pivotal moment when she had been sitting on the edge of the bed saying, "If we don't go for couples' therapy, I am leaving."

EMPTY NESTERS

Today, as I followed them through the living room and into a familiar den, I wondered how the Sternbergs were faring these many years later. When we were seated, David told me that in the last six months he had "pretty much retired." Then he smiled, as if he had said something funny.

I knew that he had spent his working life in a variety of entrepreneurial activities and been extremely successful. Indeed, the Sternbergs were, I suspected, among the wealthier couples in my sample of interviewees. "Why are you smiling?" I asked him, curiously.

"Well, I suspect that if you'd asked me about this some six months ago, I'd have gone into a long discussion about how I might be interested in a new investment project if something interesting happened to come up," he replied. "But that's probably because the word 'retirement' connotes for me—and I think for a moderate number of men . . ." He left his sentence unfinished, then shrugged as if to say that "to retire" meant that an important part of a man's life was ended.

After a few moments he added, as if musing aloud, "There are a lot of business associates that I lost touch with when I moved on. And I really don't miss them. Now my joy is to be with Nancy, to spend time with my grandchildren. . . . At the same time I'm searching for something—some project that I can give my time and my money and my brain to. Because my brain is very active and creative, and it's just constantly in my face. It still functions! And I would love to be able to use that creativity for people who would really get something out of it—something that would make their lives a little better. Whether it's a place to sleep or better health care or even a way to assure they're getting their medication—" He broke off and fell silent.

At last I looked at Nancy questioningly, as if to say, "What about you?"

She told me that she had retired from her twenty-five-hour-per-week job as a chemist some years earlier, but to this day she continued to handle the bills and keep the books on David's various enterprises.

"I decided to quit that outside job after my breast cancer was diagnosed," she stated.

That remark hung in the air. I waited for her to elaborate further upon it, but she didn't.

Instead, she began talking animatedly about having experienced a tremendous change in her life, one that had taken place over the course of the past decade. "At this point I'm free to a great degree of my own obligations and headaches with the children—and of the relationships of father and sons and father and daughter." It was as if she'd been responsible not only for her own interactions with their growing children but for overseeing David's relations with them as well.

I nodded, saying that once one's grown children had been launched, they were not so central a focus.

David leaned forward, elbows on knees. "Yes, if there's an issue or a problem that's getting me worked up, I can remove myself—disentangle myself from it for a couple of weeks till the thing cools down. The other, less negative aspect of all of this has to do with my tremendous enjoyment of the children—of the kids and of our grandchildren, too." There was a sense of deep pleasure in his voice.

Nancy then said that she believed there was a qualitative difference between couples who have had children and those who have never done so. "In one case you are two people living alone; then you are a family living together; then you are two people again. In the other case you are just two people, all along."

Once again I nodded my agreement, saying that one of the most exacting, compelling jobs of adulthood is that of rearing and launching a family. "At a certain point in time, though, that parenting job veers off from the center of attention."

I paused, looked directly into Nancy's clear green-flecked eyes and asked her if the children's leaving had been hard on her. Had she gone through a bad time or simply set about enjoying the added freedom?

"I missed them," Nancy said simply. "I was never the kind of mother who couldn't wait for her kids to leave. At the same time, David and I have enough of our own stuff going on, and we're fortunate that we can go where we want to go when we want to go. And we *do*," she added with a smile. "For instance, the two of us go biking up in Maine. We go to Acadia National Park and we bike there for days. And we'll stay at a nice hotel near the water—we do things like that."

Had her relationship with David changed significantly in the years since the kids' departure? I asked.

Nancy, without hesitating, said that their relationship had changed a great deal because their children were no longer living with them. "Most of the conflict we struggled with boiled down to issues with the kids. This kind of thing can still flare up, but it's much less pressing because they're not here. So if there's something going on and we're on opposite sides of the problem and they walk through the door, why, then we'd have to deal with it. But as it is, I think ours is an easier relationship because those pressures are at a distance, somewhat out there. They're not entirely absent, but they are much more removed."

"All told, how do you feel about the job you did as parents, plus and minus?" I asked her.

They turned to look at each other for a moment, then Nancy turned back to me. "I think we did a hell of a good job," she said. "I mean, we have *good* kids. We brought them through a lot of turmoil—it was especially rough on Greg, as the oldest—but at least we knew enough to get therapy for him."

She paused briefly, then went on to say that she was very proud of her children and felt blessed that they were the kind of people they were. "David and I did a lot of screwy things, and we had a lot of problems, but our children are really fine people. I mean, they are moral, they are ethical, they have the instinct to do the right things at the right times. And they do."

My thought, at that moment, was that the Sternbergs' children—now middle-aged, with kids of their own—must have weathered all the commotion going on in the household because at some deep level they'd felt loved and cared about.

At this point, David chimed in. "As we've gotten older, and the children have moved out of the space they took up in Nancy's life—and as I've removed myself from the space that working took up in my life—we two have become so close. So close together, in the way we think, in the way we resolve problems. Now we work them out down to almost the last detail. Yes, there is still a button that can be pushed, and then you can get me going." He stopped, laughed, shook his head as if to shake away an embarrassing recollection. "But the intensity of my reactions and the way I used to walk around feeling justified in making these irrational statements—that's *gone*. I used to tell Nancy, 'You don't understand life, because you're not out there in the real world, dealing with all these animals,' but that was just a tool I used to defend my behavior. These days, I use it almost never, because I *enjoy* seeing Nancy happy. When Nancy is happy, I'm happy. And at times when I'm getting a little whacked out in my head—which does happen—I'm able to *hear* Nancy in a way I was never able to before."

Nancy nodded. "I would talk, but he just wasn't able to take in what I was saying."

I looked from one to the other of the Sternbergs, so changed from the couple I'd interviewed years earlier. At that time their relationship had improved significantly in the wake of two years of joint therapy. They had worked hard to break the hold of their individual pasts on what was happening between them in the present, and both felt they had come a long, long way. Still, I had the feeling that there was always a simmering disagreement between them, one that might surface at any wrong turn in the conversation. It could be about sex, it could be about money, it could be about the children or the way the bathroom towels had been folded.

Now the whole sense of what was going on in these partners' lives was different, and I suppose I should not have found it surprising. I had seen this shift toward what researcher Laura Carstensen calls "positivity" in other older couples from the original sample I'd first interviewed so many years earlier. Nevertheless, it felt to me as if one of life's quiet dramas was taking place here. And as I sat there, what came to my mind was a visual image of that marital U-curve described earlier—the one that demonstrates marital satisfaction rising in tandem with the children's timely departures. The Sternbergs were clearly finding the "empty nest" they now shared to be freer and more satisfying and rewarding than the nest the two of them had shared before.

"So I'm hearing the two of you saying that the mood-tone of your life is a pretty happy one now," I said. It was a statement but also a question, and they nodded in unison.

"Oh yes, for sure," David said definitively.

CANCER

In my usual interview with an over-fifty couple, I would typically raise some fairly sticky questions close to the outset of the conversation. These had to do with the existence of any health problems that either was experiencing; with their thoughts about mortality; with their contemplation (this was always present) of the potential loss of the spouse. But in this particular instance, the mention of Nancy's breast disease—and the knowledge that her mother had died from the same illness—led me to avoid these highly sensitive issues and wait for a discussion of her breast cancer to arise spontaneously.

This didn't occur until close to the end of our joint interview, when I asked, "What do you think are the major sexual issues that arise at this time of life?" As always, this question was greeted by an extended pause, during which I maintained a carefully neutral expression on my face.

Nancy turned to her husband, said, "I don't think we have any particularly difficult issues, do we?" But then, without waiting for his response, she said, "David went through a period when he had a problem because of his medications. And these needed to be fidgeted around with for a while."

I asked her if the problem had had to do with the use of antidepressants. It is now common knowledge that the SSRIs (such as Prozac and Zoloft) can have devastating effects on a person's sexuality. But Nancy shook her head, saying that the problem had been related to a medicine for blood pressure. "Actually, he's still taking the same medication, so I don't know what that's about. Maybe his body adjusted to it, I don't know," she said with a shrug of her shoulders. "And I had a hysterectomy, because having a uterus didn't matter to me. I just got rid of everything; I had all the rest taken out. I had had breast cancer; I don't want ovarian cancer; I don't want cervical cancer. But this affected absolutely nothing."

"You had the hysterectomy electively, and not because there was something suspicious?" I asked.

"No, there wasn't a medical reason. But then, we never really knew where my mother's initial site was, and I thought it might have been ovarian. That's a really sneaky cancer that you aren't likely to catch until it's too late. So who knows? I didn't want to be bothered. That's the reason I had bilateral mastectomies, too—so I wouldn't be faced with another breast cancer. I wasn't planning to have any more kids, so my decision was just 'scoop me out.' "

As a woman, I knew how big a decision this had been. Nancy's story brought to my mind the decision of a gynecologist friend of mine whose mother and other close female relatives had all developed breast cancer. My friend had elected to have a preventative double mastectomy, and indeed, afterward, the pathologist had found a malignant tumor deep within her breast tissue.

"So I don't know," Nancy continued, turning to David again. "Do you think we have sexual issues?"

He shook his head. "We don't have issues. And a lot of that is due to our having a relationship where we can talk things through. I had that period where I had a lot of problems with using Lipitor and Zetia. And it was hard to figure out where the difficulties were coming from, because you don't know what the cause is unless you take yourself off a particular drug. One person can have a reaction that another person doesn't get at all. And with a personality like mine, I get to thinking and to overthinking, especially in the sexual area. So you know that's going to cause a problem, especially since the man has to do something in order to perform. He can't fake it."

I nodded; physically speaking, the male body—especially the aging male body—doesn't always cooperate with its owner's intentions. Had they tried any of the new drugs, such as Viagra? I asked. Nancy shook her head, saying that it was not a good option for a person with blood pressure problems (and a history of heart attack, I recalled silently).

I began to talk about the many medications that affect sex—the antidepressants, the beta blockers.

"There is no magic pill that cures everything," David intervened to say. "But no, we don't have a problem these days. We don't use any of those enhancers, but still, everything works fine and fairly frequently."

Nancy, two spots of pink appearing on her cheeks, nodded in agreement.

There was a short silence, after which David asked quietly if, during our previous interviews, they had ever talked to me about Nancy's surgery.

I shook my head, saying that it must have happened after those interviews were completed.

"Well, let's talk about it now," he said, meeting my gaze and holding it squarely. He paused briefly, then said, "It was a very tough, tricky decision, because her breasts were beautiful, and it was a matter of deciding whether to remove one breast or two. The surgeon—a woman surgeon who is also a friend of ours—called us on a Friday night and said, 'Hey, you have to tell me whether it's one breast or two, because we have to reserve the operating room for a certain number of hours.' So we sat there on that Friday night and we talked and talked . . . and about three o'clock in the morning, Nancy looked at me and said, 'You'd better enjoy them tonight, because they're not going to be here much longer.' I remember hugging and kissing her and saying, 'It's not a problem, we'll find other ways, other places. There are other things I've always fantasized doing. You know we will work at it. I will always love you.' And the surgery . . ."

I felt tears starting to my eyes. "You're going to make me cry," I said.

David held up both palms, as if to halt any traffic of this sort. "No, no, because it is so clear in my own mind when I see the love and the relationship and the friendship that we have. I remember when she came home—and to understand this you have to know that my father wanted, in the worst way, for me to be a doctor. If not a doctor, he said, he could still tolerate a son who was a dentist. But the first day I went to premed they showed a film of an eye operation, and I sat there for fifteen minutes. Then I was out of there; I was gone, and I said, 'This is not going to happen, ever.' " He laughed and shook his head.

David's few other medical encounters had happened to him when he was a camp counselor. On several occasions campers had accidents going off diving boards and had cut their heads open. "Horrible injuries! But I would pick the kid up, put him in the car, drive him twenty miles to the nearest hospital and carry him in. I put him in the doctor's arms. Then I walked outside and puked my heart out immediately."

This history, David recounted, had frightened him when he'd first brought Nancy home after the surgery. How would he respond when confronted with the wound that now existed in the place where her beautiful breasts had once been? "The nurses had told me I had to change the dressing, and they'd explained how to do it, and I said to myself, 'What am I going to do? How am I going to handle this?'

"That first day after we came home, I sat her down on the toilet seat, and I was smiling and joking while I took off the wrapping, and at the same time telling myself, 'Don't get sick, don't throw up. Just go ahead it with it.' And I did, and it was all so . . ." He stopped, raised both arms in the air, palms open as if to embrace or welcome someone.

"It was all so . . . ?" I prompted him.

"It was all so *easy*. And I said, 'Is this okay?' She said it was, and then she went back to bed and we had the pillows propped up behind her, and we just sat there and talked. I remember telling her that it was so easy, it was just so *okay*. So we worked through that," David concluded.

Later, he told me in an individual follow-up interview that in a curious way Nancy's breast cancer had been rewarding, for it made him understand how much he loved her. "I never wanted anything to do with medicine or doctoring, but I found I could change the dressing and do all the other stuff I needed to do to take care of her. And I was so proud of myself for that."

"I can see that," I said. Then I asked, my voice hesitant, "So would you say that her cancer has actually affected your relationship positively?"

"Yes, I would say that it has," he replied without hesitating.

I made no reply, but thought about the mortality statistic—one that has been duplicated over and over again since the founding of the field of sociology in the early nineteenth century—to the effect that married people live longer. And as I listened to this story, I could certainly understand that there were reasons why this should be so.

THE SMARTEST MOVE, THE DUMBEST MOVE

In a joint interview, I asked the Sternbergs the following question: "What was the smartest move, and the dumbest move, that each of you ever made?"

David leaped in to respond that the smartest move he'd ever made was to single out and then marry Nancy. However, instead of stopping after having made that assertion, he went into a long and exceedingly detailed account of how their relationship had gotten under way.

The first time he saw her was when he'd visited at a summer camp where he had formerly been a senior counselor. He described her blond hair and the black bathing suit she had been wearing; and how, later on in that afternoon, after he'd been chewed out by the baseball coach for having dropped a fly ball, she'd come over and talked with him consolingly. As he went on and on, Nancy rolled her eyes at me, as if to say she was in sympathy; enough of a good thing was enough. But David didn't notice. He went on to describe the entire series of encounters they'd had in the weeks that followed.

In a way, this recitation was endearing; but in another it was tedious, like being asked to look at a large album full of photographs of someone else's early courtship.

When her husband had finished, I turned to Nancy, asked her about the smartest move that she had ever made. I fully expected her to say something about hooking up with David.

But a troubled expression crossed her face. "Let me tell you the dumbest move first. It was when my mother was dying. Not talking to her about what was really going on and allowing her to deal with what was happening. Because those were the days when you didn't tell people."

"You didn't speak with her about it?" I asked.

She shook her head. "You weren't supposed to tell the patient because it would make the person depressed. And so the family suffered alone, and the patient suffered alone; and you all did it along parallel lines. Now my mother was more than smart enough, and more than capable enough, to have dealt with it head-on; but she really was stymied from doing that. So it was one of those things where my father knew that she knew, but she didn't want him to know that she knew, so she acted like she believed that he didn't know." Nancy's eyes were moist.

"And you yourself were involved in that triangle," David said.

"Yes, I was," she admitted. "But remember, I was twenty-five, twenty-six years old, and my father was telling me that the doctor said it wasn't good for my mother to know, and so we weren't going to tell her. I cooperated with that, but in retrospect, it was a stupid, callous thing to do . . . and I have always regretted going along."

"Because you didn't get to say the right good-bye?" I asked her quietly.

"Because I didn't allow her to express what was clearly on her mind," Nancy replied. "And I think there were a lot of things she would have said and dealt with, had she been able, but that decision just walled her in. When it comes to dumb moves, that's by far the worst one that comes to my mind." She paused.

As for the smartest thing she'd ever done, she continued, "I want to say it was linking up with David; but I don't know if that qualifies as smart. It was more like one of those blink things. It was on such a gut level that I don't know whether 'smart' is a part of that. It *was* smart, but it wasn't an act of intelligence."

It was now David's turn to answer the question about the dumbest move he had ever made. He rubbed his chin, said thoughtfully, "It's interesting that Nancy's mother was the focus of her sadness. Because as I've gotten older, I've begun to wish that I'd only had the strength to confront my father verbally. I would have liked to question him about why he felt the way he did. I would have liked to say, 'Don't you understand what my efforts are about? Don't you understand where my goodness is?' I know this is just a fantasy. It's just that I would have wanted so much to *know* him—know the man who could give so much money to charities, and who did it so secretively. We never talked adult-to-adult, the way I talk with my sons and my son-in-law. I would have liked to know what my father had inside him, and for twenty years I knew exactly what I wanted to say to him—things about what *I* wanted from the relationship. Which might very well have been rejected. He might have said, 'I don't go there,' or 'I have enough on my mind.' "

There was a long silence, which was ended by Nancy saying empathetically, "He was not an introspective person, David."

David nodded and agreed that, yes, his father probably would have cut him off if he had tried.

TAKING TIME SERIOUSLY

In an individual follow-up interview, Nancy Sternberg told me that what bothered her most about getting older was that there was less future time to go. "I'm sixty-six years old, and ten years ago I was fifty-six years old—a significantly younger person than someone in her mid-sixties. And as for those ten years between fifty-six and sixty-six—I don't know where the hell they went. And the years from sixty-six to seventy-six will probably go even faster. Because each year that you live represents a greater portion of what's to come than what's already behind you. So I know that the next ten years are probably going to go even faster than the last ten. And then there is the ten after that." She shrugged, laughed. "You know, my definition of a 'senior' citizen is now much older."

I nodded, talked about the huge, recent change in longevity. "People stay healthier, live longer. The life cycle has been expanded."

Nancy shook her head, as if to say that wasn't quite what she meant. "Here's what I think about the whole idea of being 'elderly.' When you read an article, and it says: 'Elderly seventy-year-old man swerves off the road,' or 'Elderly woman of sixty-five held up in parking lot,' I say to myself, 'Oh my God! That's not *my* definition of "elderly." ' Okay, the years between fifty-six and sixty-six are now gone—they went like smoke in the wind. So my definition of 'elderly' is now seventy-six instead of sixty-six. And it's going to advance the further along I get." She laughed. "That's not to say I would like to go back and relive the early years, but that maybe I would like to have *ten years* of being sixty-six. And maybe *ten years* of being sixty-seven and *ten years* of being sixty-eight. . . . I just wish there were some way of slowing the clock down."

She paused, then added seriously, "I just feel so reluctant to leave this period of my life."

Later, in a one-on-one interview, David Sternberg expressed sentiments that were similar. He talked about the pleasure he took in this time of life, about the fact that "we are two people in an equal deal" and not a man and a woman in an ongoing, futile quarrel over who is in control of the relationship.

"Right now, we're basically trying to figure out how we can get the most out of every day. The two of us are active, we're constantly on the move. We go on vacations with the kids. We go up to Maine, we go down to Charleston; we just spent three weeks in Florida. We really enjoy each other's company, we have a lot of fun together," he said, sounding enthused.

Then he paused. "As far as the challenges of getting older are concerned"—his voice was quieter, thoughtful, even solemn—"for me, at least—in the background—there is always an awareness of the limitations of mortality. That's *the* main challenge," he said.

Yet at the same time, I thought, it is the awareness of mortality that makes life's afternoon so ripely poignant and so sweet.

EPILOGUE

I t's true, life can change in a minute. That morning in May, there was a hillside of red tulips waving hello out in the garden. It was the day after a big birthday celebration in my honor, and the gaily decorated tent we'd rented for the party (in case it rained, but it didn't) was still standing, its tassels shifting in the breeze. We'd gone outside to have coffee and stand gazing at the empty tables and chairs that had been filled with old friends, new friends, our daughters and their husbands. We were still feeling exuberant, sharing amusing anecdotes about the evening before.

The phone started ringing, and we went back into the house. There were calls to thank us, to gossip a bit, to talk the party over. Then we went upstairs, and I began getting dressed in the bedroom. My husband was across the way, in our small upstairs sitting room, and I was in the middle of telling him a long story, when I heard a loud crash. "What happened?" I called. There was no reply. It sounded like a floor lamp or a heavy chair had fallen over. But what, exactly, was it?

"Herb?" I called again, but again there was no answer. At first that didn't really alarm me. The walls in our house are old and thick, and we often don't hear each other unless we are fairly close by. Perhaps my husband had gone downstairs; but then, what was that loud noise about? No, he must be upstairs, and must have knocked something over—something that sounded big. But what could it have been?

"Herb?" This time my voice was much louder, and held a note of anxiety. Still, there was nothing but silence. Where was he? I raised my voice again, calling his name, then went across the hall to look for him. There I found his unconscious body, slumped against the bottom of the sitting-room door. What had just happened? Hadn't we been joking and chatting about the birthday party a minute or two earlier?

How could it be that in this tiny interval of time he had fallen—fainted?—and crashed into the door frame on his way down? This scene seemed unreal, something that partook of the fantastic. I leaned over him, repeating his name. He didn't hear me. He was alive, his eyelids were fluttering, but he wasn't conscious. I held his head, tried breathing air into his mouth, alternately calling his name over and over. I was attempting mouth-to-mouth resuscitation, barely remembered from my camp counseling days; but I wasn't sure I was doing it the right way, nor was I sure that it was what was needed in this crisis situation.

It was clear that Herb couldn't hear me, but I kept calling his name. Was I in a state of terror? Actually, "terror" doesn't capture what I was experiencing. I was in a place for which no words exist—a place beyond space and time, a world gone vacant with suspense. I felt like a trapeze artist whirling high up in the empty air, uncertain about whether there will be any waiting rope to grab on to, or any hand to reach out and swing her forward to a safe landing. It was white noise, a screen gone blank, a sense of prolonged, breathless tension during which life is without motion and the outcome hangs in the balance.

"Herb! Herb!" His eyes kept fluttering in that unseeing way, but he wasn't responding to my voice. I wanted to run to the telephone and call 911 but was afraid to leave him, even for a moment. I thought he might be dying, and I couldn't leave him alone. So I kept doing what I was doing—calling his name, breathing into his mouth—even though it didn't seem to be working.

Some minutes later (I'm not sure how many) his eyes finally opened. He looked at me, his expression puzzled, and asked me what had happened. I told him that I didn't know, but I was calling an ambulance. He seemed befuddled, told me not to go to the trouble. *Trouble?* I didn't listen to this diffident suggestion, and twenty minutes later we were in the emergency room of the Yale–New Haven hospital. He had been taken there by ambulance; I had followed him in my car. The doctors on call ordered a series of tests, and soon ruled out the two most threatening possibilities—it wasn't a heart attack, it wasn't a stroke. One of our daughters joined me an hour later. We waited and waited. He was lying on a gurney in a hallway; we were waiting for a room. Finally, by nightfall of that beautiful day in May, a bed—and an explanation—became available.

Bottom line, the problem had been caused by a doctor's misjudgment. Herb had been on a medication for his mildly elevated blood pressure, but the pill was working much too well. His pulse rate had dipped to the low forties. He had complained about this to his physician, but had been told that this was not a cause for concern. However, it was. Herb's passing out and hitting the door frame (which then led to a hip operation) had been caused by a dangerously slow heartbeat. In fact, he'd blanked out once before, very briefly, when we were driving on a superhighway. So we were *both* lucky to be alive.

I was grateful for that, but still, for me, this was the "buzzer" incident that Jackie Winston later talked about during our interviews. When she said of her husband's amnesia, "It was like a little gong or buzzer sounding, for both of us. It was a buzzer saying, 'Yes, it's time to check this out. You're at a different place in your life,' " I knew exactly what she was talking about.

It was simply happenstance that during this period I was beginning to look through the research on couples over fifty. I was particularly interested in writings about those older adults whom gerontologists call the "young-old." This is the large group of relatively healthy, active people between fifty and seventy-five years of age—a group that was minuscule in the early 1900s, when life expectancy was roughly age fifty, but which has grown exponentially during the course of the twentieth century.

It was clear that something phenomenal had occurred: twenty-five to thirty years had been added to the life span, and yet I was finding the research on this phenomenon frustratingly sketchy. It was true that the newer books and papers on aging had changed in tone. They were no longer focused on themes such as social disengagement, loneliness, depletion and deterioration, but on subjects such as "productive aging," "aging well," "successful aging" and the like. However, I was coming away from all my reading with disjointed kinds of information, rather than with an overarching theoretical focus.

For instance, I learned the odd fact that individuals who had valued older people early in their own lives tended to enjoy a life span that was some seven years longer. Interesting: this suggested that self-esteem affected mortality. Then again, I was reading about how that period of post-work leisure called retirement—usually thought of as a onetime life event: now you're working, now you're not—had morphed into a situation in which "retirement" might be followed by a second full-time career, part-time employment or a new, home-based business. Older adults were being resourceful, and a number of them were finding ways to turn what formerly had been a hobby into a paying concern.

I was also reading a wide, and widely divergent, array of scholarly papers and books with titles such as: "Do Attitudes Toward Divorce Affect Marital Quality?"; "Optimism, Pessimism, and the Desire for Longer Life"; "Age Integration and the Lives of Older People"; and *Epidemiology and Aging*. I was particularly astonished by one research work carried out by Chicago sociologist Linda J. Waite et al. It was called "Does Divorce Make People Happy?" and I knew I would want to write about this remarkable study eventually. Meanwhile, in a long, fairly dry treatise on aging I came across a striking statistic, one that I was unable to get out of my mind thereafter.

It was the curious finding that older people who got into an auto accident had typically been struck from the left side. The book's authors suggested that the cause might be attributed to losses in peripheral vision. But the upshot was that every time my husband and I came to a stop sign, I would say, "Look out! Death comes from the left!" I was joking, but nevertheless Herb soon learned that he had to come to a complete stop even if there was no other car in sight.

During this period of reading and interviewing, I was not only talking to experts in the field of aging but beginning to interview couples in the fifty-plus age group as well. These long, probing conversations

were moving me into an unanticipated, somewhat confusing terrain.
The purpose of my project was to find out how these older partners
were experiencing the "gift" of the newly elongated life cycle, but the
interviews were turning out to be different from anything I'd imagined. I had expected to hear dirges about health; fears about impending retirement; worries about the need to relocate; complaints about
ungrateful adult children and about increasingly strained, problematic marriages. But the couples I was talking with sounded relatively
happy. Most of them exuded a sense of contentment and well-being—
including some partners who'd been tense and argumentative twenty
years earlier, when I'd interviewed them for my book *Intimate Partners*.
I was encountering a phenomenon I didn't understand.

I talked this over with a close friend of mine, Julie, who is a sea-
soned therapist, and I told her I needed to find some unhappy over-
fifty couples somewhere. Otherwise, my book would lack realistic
balance and have a Pollyanna-like tone.

"Interview me," she said. "My marriage is a mess."

Surprised and taken aback, I asked her if her husband would agree
to this. She said she knew he would, and we set a date—a Sunday
afternoon, because Ed is a busy practicing lawyer.

"Make sure that you two are having a *bad* day," I said facetiously, as
the two of us paid our lunch bill and parted.

"Don't worry," she said. "Every day is a bad day."

However, when the interview took place, in their Fairfield,
Connecticut, home, I was in for a disappointment. We sat in their
modern living room on white, nubby love seats, facing one another.
As the conversation proceeded, I noticed that these partners bantered
easily and met each other's eyes fairly often. I was struck by the fact
that the pair of them could have passed as brother and sister. Both

Julie and Ed are rail-thin and have hazel eyes and gray-flecked curly dark hair.

At one point, when I came to the question "What do you think were the smartest and the dumbest moves you ever made in your life?" Ed didn't hesitate before saying feelingly, "The smartest move I ever made in my life was marrying Julie." That statement ended all conversation for a few moments.

I looked at Julie to gauge her reaction. Her eyes were brimming with tears. She turned to gaze at her husband wordlessly. My own thought was that I might as well turn off my recorder. No matter how Julie might characterize their relationship, she and her husband had flunked the "impossible marriage" exam.

In time, I spoke with Morton Reiser, a distinguished psychoanalyst and neuroscientist. He told me that of course older couples are happier, because, generally speaking, older *individuals* are happier. This, he said, is due to brain changes associated with aging: a certain region of the brain, the locus coeruleus (which means "blue spot"), loses nerve cells as we grow older. "The locus coeruleus is associated with depression, panic disorders and anxiety," Dr. Reiser explained. "So it's no wonder that people begin feeling better as they age." Later, I was to find that other brain areas are affected as we age, and with similarly benign results.

But it was a fortuitous conversation with psychologist Peter Salovey, dean of the College of Arts and Sciences at Yale University, that finally pointed me in what was to become an extremely fruitful direction. He suggested that I contact Dr. Laura Carstensen at Stanford University, and for the first time I encountered an overarching theoretical perspective that could explain the heightened sense of satisfaction and well-being I was meeting in the course of my interviews. I learned, from conversations with Dr. Carstensen and from research work carried out at the Life-span Laboratory she directs, that while older adults may experience certain age-associated impairments—such as losses in memory, reaction timing, vision and the like—they experience no handicap whatsoever when it comes to the domain of emotional processing and emotional control. In fact, they may show some improvement.

Carstensen's theory, based on solid experimental research, is that as we age we are ever more aware of the ticking clock moving us closer to life's ending. We take time very seriously. And, as a result, we behave in ways that will enhance the satisfying, intimate, benign relationships in our lives and keep the toxic ones at a distance. In brief, older adults are proactive: they do things that will encourage positive happenings in their lives as instinctively as sunflowers lean toward the sun.

As I read through Carstensen's papers, I had the odd feeling that I'd unexpectedly caught sight of myself in a mirror. This focus on what she called "positivity" was exactly what had been going on in my own life. For example, there were a couple of people in my world who left me feeling disconcerted whenever we met or talked. And, in both cases, I'd recently done what had earlier seemed unthinkable. Figuratively speaking, I had put down my tennis racket and walked off the court. I'd simply arrived at the realization that if one player failed to return the other's serve, these unrewarding, ungratifying interactions could not continue.

Throughout this period, my intensive interviews with over-fifty couples were ongoing. I had a fixed set of open-ended questions that I asked every couple, and though their responses varied widely, they were telling me that the news was on the bright side. For example, couples like the McBrides and the Sternbergs might at one point in their married lives have seemed doomed to go on repeating the same distressing interpersonal scenarios. But these partners had been able to introduce novelty—something new and happier—into an intimate relationship that once seemed hopelessly stuck in a rigid, ungratifying pattern. They, and other couples in my sample, were showing me that change—even radical transformation—is possible at every phase of the life cycle.

I was impressed, as well, by a subtheme that emerged in so many of these structured conversations. This was the fact that many of my interviewees had been able to find creative outlets in their later years—ways of remaining engaged that offered their lives meaning, purpose and direction.

I was also learning some surprising things about sex in the older adult years. Partners like the Donaldsons and the Winstons, whose sexual activities had slowed down, might have been concerned about this fact but were nevertheless basking in contented, close, deeply satisfying relationships. And couples like the Hamiltons, who were clearly devoted to each other, taught me that the lack of genital sexual relationships in the marriages of people in their later years is not necessarily a tragic outcome. I was, on the other hand, touched by the intimate sexual relationship that the Sternbergs continued to enjoy in the wake of Nancy's traumatic breast cancer operation. However, though sex is a perennially interesting topic, I could not make a defining statement about sexuality in older adulthood, aside from the observation that it doesn't appear to be as crucial as real *affection* between the members of the pair.

All in all, the message I took away from this research and these many interviews was that life is not seamlessly perfect in the later years. Rather, it is that people at this phase of their lives have a different relationship to what is *not* perfect—including what is not perfect about the beloved Other.

Often, one question that was part of my format—"How have your arguments changed over time?"—evoked laughter on the part of the couple, and a wry admission that their arguments *hadn't* changed in terms of what was being argued about. What *was* different was the presence of humor and the level of intensity involved. I found myself laughing along with them, knowing that if my husband and I were the interviewees, our responses would have been similar.

As the British psychoanalyst Henry V. Dicks once famously observed, the basic truth about marriage is that it is—due to its combination of sensuality and intense emotionality—the nearest adult equivalent to the mother-child relationship. The very experience of falling in love has to do with summoning up the inchoate, rapturous feelings of being engulfed in the safe and intimate world of early infancy. This is the world of the so-called Golden Fantasy—a world in which two are one, perfect company, and where perfect nurturance exists. It has to do with a vision of Eden, buried within us, before our basic human separateness has been perceived—the realization that each one of us has been born, and will die, alone.

And it has to do, inevitably, with expulsion from that Golden Fantasy—the dream of living in a state of endless, unfailing mutual merger. For eventually, those reawakened fantasies of perfect oneness bring in their train memories of disappointments and old alarms,

deep-seated fears of separation, loss and/or abandonment. It is in marriage that we resurrect not only the intensity of our earliest attachment
feelings but also the miseries of old frustrations and resentments.
These things happen in intimate relationships, for we fall in love with
those to whom we spontaneously resonate—those who are, at some
subliminal level, deeply familiar. As marital theorists know, what is
so frequently sought in a mate—and then fought out with the mate—
is some dilemma dating from the distant past, in the original family,
that has never been fully resolved.

But what I have found, in my own marriage and in the marriages of
the many older partners I have interviewed, is an ease and a readiness
to address the inevitable misunderstandings and hurt feelings that are
inherent in any long-lasting intimate partnership; and to do so with
greater patience, compassion, humor and the vastly moderating filter
of the long view.

"Life is sweet," one thoughtful interviewee, a man in his late sixties,
told me. "Realistically speaking, it's not that I don't have occasional
feelings of frustration in my relationship; but those feelings are far, far
less intense than they were in the past. I may still have some ambivalence, but my relationship to that ambivalence has changed completely."

As someone at this stage of life, and in a long marriage, I agree. Life
is not unequivocally glorious, but it is pretty darn good.

ACKNOWLEDGMENTS

My heartfelt thanks go to Dr. Jesse Geller, Ph.D., associate clinical professor of psychiatry at Yale, who first assured me that there truly *was* a book to be written on the subject of older couples, and that I was the very person to do it. I would also like to add that in the course of a long and important association, he has always been *there* for me—a kind, patient guide, and the smartest, most perceptive of mentors. To be frank, I find it hard even to imagine what the long process of interviewing, researching and writing about later-adult couples would have been like without Jesse Geller's astute, discerning and supportive presence throughout. I am deeply, deeply grateful to him.

I am also profoundly obliged to Dr. Laura Carstensen, director of Stanford University's Life-span Development Laboratory, whose brilliant papers and helpful conversations have come to constitute the very heart of this book. Many thanks are also due to Dr. Linda Waite, the Lucy Flower Professor in Urban Sociology at the University of Chicago, whose startling research on the aftermath of divorce—and whose helpful talks with this author—turned many of my fixed beliefs on marriage and marital breakup completely upside down. I surely owe a debt of gratitude to Professor David Ekerdt, director of the Gerontology Center at the University of Kansas, for the patience he showed during our many discussions of the ways in which retirement pensions have changed over the course of time. Thanks are also due to Professor Ekerdt for our fascinating conversation about the widespread (but false) conviction that there is a link between retirement and declining health, and for his remarkable research on this subject.

I am also indebted to Dr. Peter Salovey, dean of the College of Arts and Sciences at Yale University, for a couple of pivotal conversations, each of which served to steer me in a tremendously favorable direction. Thanks, too, to sociologist Andrew Cherlin, the Benjamin H. Griswold, III, Professor of Public Policy at Johns Hopkins University, who knew the answer to every single question I ever asked him! I am grateful to the distinguished composer Martin Bresnick for intuitively translating the entire notion of this project into a perfect musical idea. Others who have shown me great help and kindness along the way are psychologist Robert Levenson, Ph.D., of the University of California; Associate Professor Janet Belsky, of the University of Tennessee; Professor Emeritus Michael Johnson, of Pennsylvania State University; Dr. Neal Cutler, a founding father of the American Institute of Financial Gerontology; Professor Mahzarin Banaji, of Harvard University, an expert in the study of ageism; psychiatrist Robert Waldinger, director of the long-running, longitudinal Grant Study at Harvard, who shared his wonderfully probing questionnaire with me; and to Dr. Judith Crowell, M.D., who devised the laser-like Current Relationship Interview section of that very fine document.

Warm thanks are due to my outstanding editor, Jake Morrisey, and to my ace of an agent, Lydia Wills. You are both smart, wonderful people to work with! A fond word of appreciation also goes to a person who has been a friend and staple of my professional life throughout, my assistant, Felicia Naumann Dickinson. She has been an integral part of my office support system for so long that I'm not sure I could go on breathing without her! The indefatigable Gokay Saher provided me with the speedy library help that is so necessary in order to maintain my forward motion. Gokay Saher also offered me his computer and PowerPoint expertise; and all the while, he helped me to keep a mountain of research papers in fairly respectable order.

Finally, when it comes to expressing my gratitude and thanks to the many couples who welcomed me into the heartland of their lives, let me confess that I find myself almost tongue-tied. All I can say is that talking with you, often admiring you, thinking incessantly about you, occasionally worrying about you, sometimes feeling jealous of you, even dreaming about you, have been some of the most remarkable experiences of my life. I felt transformed, by the end of this project; and, perhaps not surprisingly, my husband did too.

—Maggie Scarf
Whitney Humanities Center, Yale University,
New Haven, Connecticut

SELECTED REFERENCES

Amato, P. R., and S. J. Rogers. "Do Attitudes Toward Divorce Affect Marital Quality?" *Journal of Family Issues* 20 (1999): 69–86.

Baltes, Paul B., and Margret M. Baltes, eds. *Successful Aging: Perspectives from the Behavioral Sciences.* Cambridge: Cambridge University Press, 1993.

Bengston, Vern, ed. *Adulthood and Aging: Research on Continuities and Discontinuities.* New York: Springer, 1996.

Blanchard-Fields, F. "Reasoning on Social Dilemmas Varying in Emotional Saliency: An Adult Developmental Perspective." *Psychology and Aging* 1(4) (Dec. 1986): 325–33.

Brandtstadter, J., and W. Greve. "The Aging Self: Stabilizing and Protective Processes." *Developmental Review* 14 (1994): 52–80.

Bushfield, S. Y., T. R. Fitzpatrick, and B. H. Vinick. "Perceptions of 'Impingement' and Marital Satisfaction Among Wives of Retired Husbands." *Journal of Gerontological Social Work* (in review).

Butler, Robert N., and Myrna I. Lewis. *Love and Sex After 60,* Revised Ed. New York: Harper and Row, 1988.

Carstensen, L. L., D. M. Isaacowitz, and S. T. Charles. "Taking Time Seriously: A Theory of Socioemotional Selectivity." *American Psychologist* 54 (1999): 165–81.

Carstensen, L. L., and J. A. Mikels. "At the Intersection of Emotion and Cognition: Aging and the Positivity Effect." *Current Directions in Psychological Science* 14 (3) (2005): 117–21.

Carstensen, L. L., H. Fung, and S. Charles. "Socioemotional Selectivity Theory and the Regulation of Emotion in the Second Half of Life." *Motivation and Emotion* 27 (2) (2003): 103–23.

Carstensen, L. L., M. Pasupathi, U. Mayr, and J. Nesselroade. Emotional Experience in Everyday Life Across the Adult Life Span. *Journal of Personality and Social Psychology* 79 (2000): 644–55.

Carstensen, L. L. "Social and Emotional Patterns in Adulthood: Support for Socioemotional Selectivity Theory." *Psychology and Aging* 7 (1992) 331–38.

Cath, S. H. "The Orchestration of Disengagement." *International Journal of Aging and Human Development* 6 (3) (1975): 199–213.

Charles, S. T., M. Mather, and L. L. Carstensen. "Aging and Emotional Memory: The Forgettable Nature of Negative Images for Older Adults." *Journal of Experimental Psychology: General* 132 (2003): 310–24.

Charles, S. T., and L. L. Carstensen. "Emotion Regulation and Aging." In James J. Gross, ed., *Handbook of Emotion Regulation.* New York: Guilford Press, 2007.

Cheng, S. T. "Age and Subjective Well-Being Revisited: A Discrepancy Perspective." *Psychology and Aging* 19 (3) (2004): 409–15.

Cherlin, A. J. "The Deinstitutionalization of American Marriage." *Journal of Marriage and Family* 66 (2004): 848–61.

Cherlin, A. J. "American Marriage in the Early Twenty-first Century." *The Future of Children* 15 (2) 2005: 33–55.

Christensen, K., and J. W. Vaupel. "Determinants of Longevity: Genetic, Environmental, and Medical Factors." *Journal of Internal Medicine* 240 (6) (Dec. 1996): 333–41.

Crimmins, E., M. D. Hayward, and Y. Saito. "Changing Mortality and Morbidity Rates and the Health Status and Life Expectancy of the Older Population." *Demography* 31 (1994): 159–75.

Crowther, M. R., M. W. Parker, W. A. Achenbaum, W. L. Larimore, and H. G. Koenig. "Rowe and Kahn's Model of Successful Aging Revisited: Positive Spirituality—the Forgotten Factor." *Gerontologist* 42 (5) (2002): 613–20.

Cutler, Neal. *Advising Mature Clients: The New Science of Wealth Span Planning.* New York: John Wiley, 2002.

Diener, E., R. A. Emmons, R. J. Larsen, and S. Griffin. "The Satisfaction with Life Scale." *Journal of Personality Assessment* 49 (1985): 71–75.

Diener, E. "Subjective Well-Being." *Psychological Bulletin* 95 (1984): 542–75.

Diener, E., and E. Suh. "Measuring Quality of Life: Economic, Social and Subjective Indicators." *Social Indicators Research* 40 (1–2) (1997): 189–216(28).

Ekerdt, D. J., L. Baden, R. Bosse, and E. Dibbs. "The Effect of Retirement on Physical Health." *American Journal of Public Health* 73 (1983): 779–83.

Ekerdt, D. J., and E. Clark. "Selling Retirement in Financial Planning Advertisements." *Journal of Aging Studies* 15 2001: 55–68.

Ekerdt, D. J. "Born to Retire: The Foreshortened Life Course." *The Gerontologist* 44 (2004): 3–9.

Ekerdt, D. J. "Why the Notion Persists That Retirement Harms Health." *Journal of Gerontology* 27 (1987): 454–57.

Ekerdt, D. J., R. Baden, R. Bosse, and E. Dibbs. "The Effect of Retirement on Physical Health." *American Journal of Public Health* 73 (1983): 779–83.

Ekerdt, D. J. "Retirement Transition." In D. J. Ekerdt et al., eds., *Encyclopedia of Aging Volume 4.* New York: Macmillan Reference USA, 2002: 1217–22.

Ekerdt, D. J., and B. H. Vinick. "Marital Complaints in Husband-Working and Husband-Retired Couples." *Research on Aging* 13 (1991): 364–82.

Erikson, E. "The Life Cycle." In *The International Encyclopedia of the Social Sciences, Volume 9,* 1976.

Erikson, E. H. *The Life Cycle Completed: A Review.* New York: Norton, 1982.

Fitzpatrick, T. R., B. H. Vinick, and S. Bushfield. "Anticipated and Experienced Changes in Activities After Husbands Retire." *Journal of Gerontological Social Work* 46 (2) (2005): 69–84.

Frenkel, E. "Studies in Biographical Psychology." *Character and Personality* (5) 1936: 1–35.

Friedan, Betty. *Fountain of Age*. New York: Simon and Schuster, 1994.

Fung, H. H., and L. L. Carstensen. "Goals Change When Life's Fragility Is Primed: Lessons Learned from Older Adults, the September 11th Attacks and SARS." *Social Cognition* 24 (2006): 248–78.

Fung, H. H., C. Rice, and L. L. Carstensen. "Reactive and Proactive Motivational Changes Across Adulthood." In W. Greve, K. Rothermund, and D. Wentura, eds. *The Adaptive Self*. New York: Hogrefe/Huber Publisher, 2005.

Gardner, J., and A. J. Oswald. "Do Divorcing Couples Become Happier by Breaking Up?" *Journal of the Royal Statistical Society: Series H* 169 (2006): 319–36.

Geller, J. A. *Breaking Destructive Patterns: Multiple Strategies for Treating Partner Abuse*. New York: The Free Press, 1992.

Gilford, R., and V. Bengston. "Measuring Marital Satisfaction in Three Generations: Positive and Negative Dimensions." *Journal of Marriage and Family* 39 (1979): 387–98.

Glenn, N. D. "Quantitative Research on Marital Quality in the 1980's: A Critical Review." *Journal of Marriage and Family* 52 (1990): 818–31.

Glenn, N. D., and S. McLanahan. "Children and Marital Happiness: A Further Specification of the Relationship." *Journal of Marriage and Family* 44 (1) (Feb. 1982): 63–72.

Gottlieb, Lori. "Marry Him!" *Atlantic Monthly* (March 2008).

Greenwald, A. G., and M. R. Banaji. (1995). "Implicit Social Cognition: Attitudes, Self-Esteem, and Stereotypes." *Psychological Review* 102 (1) (1995): 4–27.

Haan, N., R. Millsap, and E. Hartka. "As Time Goes By: Change and Stability in Personality Over Fifty Years." *Psychology and Aging* 1 (3) (Sep. 1986): 220–32.

Hardy, M. A. "The Transformation of Retirement in Twentieth-Century America: From Discontent to Satisfaction." *Generations* 26 (2) (2002): 9–16.

Harris, Louis. *Aging in the Eighties : America in Transition—A Survey*. Washington, D.C.: National Council on the Aging, 1981.

Hetherington, E. Mavis, and John Kelly. *For Better or for Worse: Divorce Reconsidered*. New York: W. W. Norton & Company, 2002.

Hjelmborg, J. V., I. Iachine, A. Skytthe, J. W. Vaupel, M. McGue, M. Koskenvuo, J. Kaprio, N. L. Pedersen, and K. Christensen. "Genetic Influence on Human Lifespan and Longevity." *Human Genetics* 119 (3) (Apr. 2006): 312–21.

Hobbs, Frank B., and Bonnie L. Damon. *65+ in the United States*. Washington, D.C.: Bureau of the Census, 1996.

Hopper, Joseph. "The Rhetoric of Motives in Divorce." *Journal of Marriage and Family* 55 (4) (Nov. 1993): 801–13.

Hymowitz, Kay S. *Marriage and Caste in America: Separate and Unequal Families in a Post-Marital Age*. Chicago: Ivan R. Dee, 2006.

Isaacowitz, D. M., H. A. Wadlinger, D. Goren, and H. R. Wilson. "Selective Preference in Visual Fixation Away from Negative Images in Old Age? An Eye-Tracking Study." *Psychology and Aging* 21 (1) (March 2006): 40–48.

Johnson, M. P., J. P. Caughlin, and T. L. Huston. "The Tripartite Nature of Marital Commitment: Personal, Moral, and Structural Reasons to Stay Married." *Journal of Marriage and Family* 61 (1) (Feb. 1999): 160–77.

Jung, C. G., Joseph Campbell, ed., R. F. C. Hull, trans. *The Portable Jung*. New York: Viking, 1971.

Kalmijn, M., and C. W. S. Monden. "Are the Negative Effects of Divorce on Well-Being Dependent on Marital Quality?" *Journal of Marriage and Family* 68 (Dec. 2006): 1197–1213.

Karp, David A. "The Social Construction of Retirement Among Professionals 50–60 Years Old." *The Gerontologist* 29 (1989): 750–60.

Kennedy, Q., M. Mather, and L. L. Carstensen. "The Role of Motivation in the Age-Related Positivity Effect in Autobiographical Memory." *Psychological Science* 15 (2004): 208–14.

Lacey, H. P., D. M. Smith, and P. A. Ubel. "Hope I Die Before I Get Old: Mispredicting Happiness Across the Life Span." *Journal of Happiness Studies* 7 (2) (June 2006): 167–82.

Lang, F. R., and L. L. Carstensen. "Close Emotional Relationships in Late Life: Further Support for Proactive Aging in the Social Domain." *Psychology and Aging* 9 (1994): 315–24.

Lang, F. R., and L. L. Carstensen. "Time Counts: Future Time Perspective, Goals and Social Relationships." *Psychology and Aging* 17 (2002): 125–39.

Lawton, M. P., M. S. Moss, L. Winter, and C. Hoffman. "Motivation in Later Life: Personal Projects and Well-Being." *Psychology and Aging* 17 (4) (Dec. 2002): 539–47.

Lee, Gary R. "Marital Intimacy Among Older Persons: The Spouse as Confidant." *Journal of Family Issues* 9 (2) (1988): 273–84.

Levenson, R. W., L. L. Carstensen, and J. M. Gottman. "Long-Term Marriage: Age, Gender and Satisfaction." *Psychology and Aging* 8 (2) (1993): 301–13.

Levenson. R. W., L. L. Carstensen, and J. M. Gottman. "The Influence of Age and Gender on Affect, Physiology, and their Interrelations: A Study of Long-Term Marriages." *Journal of Personality and Social Psychology* 67 (1) (July 1994): 56–68.

Levy, B. R., and M. R. Banaji. "Implicit Ageism." In Todd D. Nelson, ed., *Ageism: Stereotyping and Prejudice Against Older Persons.* Cambridge, MA: The MIT Press, 2002.

Lindau, S. T., L. P. Schumm, E. O. Laumann, W. Levinson, C. A. O'Muircheartaigh, and L. J. Waite. "A Study of Sexuality and Health Among Older Adults in the United States." *The New England Journal of Medicine* 357 (2007): 762–74.

Lindberg, C., and L. L. Carstensen. "Emotions and Emotional Stability." In W. S. Markides, ed., *Encyclopedia of Health and Aging.* Thousand Oaks, CA: Sage Publications, 2007: 190–92.

Mather, M., and L. L. Carstensen. "Aging and Motivated Cognition: The Positivity Effect in Attention and Memory." *Trends in Cognitive Sciences* 9 (2005) 496–502.

Midanik, L. T., K. Soghikian, L. J. Ransom, and I. S. Tekawa. "The Effect of Retirement on Mental Health and Health Behaviors: The Kaiser Permanente Retirement Study." *Journals of Gerontology Series B: Psychological Sciences and Social Sciences* 50 (1995): S59–S61.

Mikels, J. A., G. R. Larkin, P. A. Reuter-Lorenz, and L. L. Carstensen. "Divergent Trajectories in the Aging Mind: Changes in Working Memory for Affective Versus Visual Information with Age." *Psychology and Aging* 20 (4) (2005): 542–53.

Mroczek, D. K., and C. M. Kolarz. "The Effect of Age on Positive and Negative Affect: A Developmental Perspective on Happiness." *Journal of Personality and Social Psychology* 75 (1998): 1333–49.

Neugarten, Bernice Levin. *Personality in Middle and Late Life: Empirical Studies.* New York: Atherton Press, 1964.

Nosek, B. A., M. B. Banaji, and A. G. Greenwald. "Harvesting Implicit Group Attitudes and Beliefs from a Demonstration Web Site." *Group Dynamics* 6 (2002): 101–15.

Vaillant, G. E., and K. Mukamal. "Successful Aging." *The American Journal of Psychiatry* 158 (June 2001): 839–47.

Vinick, B. H., and D. J. Ekerdt. "Retirement: What Happens to Husband-Wife Relationships?" *Journal of Geriatric Psychiatry* 24 (1) (1991): 23–40.

Waite, Linda, ed. *Does Divorce Make People Happy?* Institute for American Values, Study. New York: 2002.

Waite, L., and Y. Luo. "Marital Happiness and Marital Stability: Consequences for Psychological Well-Being." Paper presented at the annual meeting of the American Sociological Association, Chicago (Aug. 2002).

Waite, Linda J., and Maggie Gallagher. *The Case for Marriage: Why Married People Are Happier, Healthier, and Better Off Financially.* New York: Doubleday, 2000.

White, L., and J. N. Edwards. "Emptying the Nest and Parental Well-Being: An Analysis of National Panel Data." *American Sociological Review* 55 (2) (Apr. 1990): 235–42.

Yalom, Marilyn, and Laura L. Carstensen, eds. *Inside the American Couple.* Berkeley, CA: University of California Press, 2002.

INDEX

abusive marriages, 64–68
adolescence
     as parenting challenge, 78
     as recent development, 10–11
     third age compared with, 11, 25, 42, 139
adult children. *See* children
affection, 24, 104, 238
Ageism (Diener and Suh), 88
aging, negative perceptions of, 12–13, 87–88,
     159–60
American Institute of Financial Gerontology
     (AIFG), 195, 197
argument. *See* conflict

baby boomers, 9–10
Baden, Lynn, 161–62
Banaji, Mahzarin, 87–88
Bengtson, Vern, 104
"bonus years." *See* third age
Bosse, Raymond, 161–62
brain function
     confusion and disorientation, 133–38
     positive changes with aging, 74, 89, 235
     transient global amnesia, 136–38
Bresnick, Martin, 5–7
Bruce, Laura, 142
Butler, Robert N., 124–25

care of elderly relatives, 71–72, 153–54,
     194
Carstensen, Laura
     on emotional processing and control,
          236
     emotions in daily life, study of, 95–98
     "Emotional Experience in Everyday Life
          Across the Adult Life Span," 98
     Inside the American Couple (Yalom and
          Carstensen), 125–26
     interactions between partners, study of,
          101–4
     life-span theory, 104
     paradox of aging, 13–14
     positivity effect theory, 95
     on sense of time, 89–91
     on sexual activity of older couples,
          125–26
     on shrinkage of social circles, 92
     socioemotional selectivity theory, 14
     "Taking Time Seriously" (Carstensen and
          Charles), 1, 90–91
Charles, Susan, 1, 91
Cherlin, Andrew, 19
children
     challenges of raising, 50, 57, 78–79, 213,
          216–17

children (*continued*)
    as consideration in divorce, 17, 53, 55
    cost of educating, 33–34, 109–10
    departure from home, 116, 121, 148,
        216, 218
    disappointment with, 80–81
    enjoyment of and satisfaction with, 21,
        36–37, 38, 59, 153, 174, 215,
        217, 227
    of single mothers, 18–19
commitment, 51–57
conflict
    affection despite, 104
    categories of problems, 50–51
    changes in approach to, 175–76, 215,
        217–18, 238, 239
    compromise and acquiescence, 81–82
    decrease in frequency and intensity of,
        103–4
    over money, 188–89
    struggle for control, 211, 212
    unresolved problems in family of origin,
        239
creativity, 111, 147, 151–52, 214, 237
Cutler, Neal, 195–97

Daignault, Cathy, 203–5
death
    anticipation of, 29–31, 197–99
    financial planning for surviving spouse,
        198, 200, 204–5
    of parent, 71, 80, 213, 219, 220, 224–25
    of sibling, 71, 80, 205, 212
Dibbs, Elaine, 161–62
Dicks, Henry V., 238
Diener, Ed, 88
disagreement. *See* conflict
disappointment, 37–41
disengagement theory, 91–92, 154
divorce
    from abusive marriage, 64–68
    and consideration of children, 17, 53, 55
    decision against, 51–57
    decision for, 41, 45
    distress of procedure, 54–55, 61–62
    in early years of marriage, 20

escape hypothesis, 61–64
rate of, 17, 19–20
rate of happy remarriage, 48
social acceptability of, 18, 55–56, 179
well-being after, 46–48, 61–64

education costs, 33–34, 109–10
Ekerdt, David
    on home mortgage interest deduction,
        144
    retirement and health, study of, 161–62
    on retirement planning, 146
    on work ethic, 160
"Emotional Experience in Everyday Life
        Across the Adult Life Span"
        (Carstensen), 98
emotional function and stability
    affection, 24, 104, 238
    benefits of close relationships, 104
    brain changes, 74, 89, 235
    in daily life, 95–98
    disengagement, 91–92, 154
    distress after divorce, 61–64
    emotional growth, 34, 177
    "eye love," 129, 209
    forgiveness, 34, 115
    improvement with age, 14, 89, 94, 103–4
    perspective on problems, 215
    positive orientation, 14, 24, 94–95, 218,
        236
    selectivity in relationships, 14, 92–94
    understanding and connection, 42, 58,
        99–101, 175–76, 217
    worry about spouse, 198
empty nest, 116, 121, 148, 216, 218
Erikson, Erik, 152–53
escape hypothesis, 61–64
"eye love," 129, 209

family genogram, 26
family of origin
    attitudes about money, 32–33
    care of elderly relatives, 71–72, 153–54,
        194
    death of parent, 71, 80, 213, 219, 220,
        224–25

death of sibling, 71, 80, 205, 212
disapproval of divorce, 179
disapproval of spouse, 112
domineering father, 211–13, 225–26
emotionally distant mother, 43, 171, 211
hostile home atmosphere, 180, 185
influence on relationship with mate,
    37–38, 239
limitations imposed by, 81–82
longevity, 70, 72–73
management of parents' finances, 72,
    205
sexualized relationship with father, 180,
    185, 207
feelings. See emotional function and stability
fights. See conflict
finances. See money and finance
financial gerontology, 195–97
forgiveness, 34, 115

Geller, Janet, 65
generativity, 152–53
genogram, 26
gerontology
    financial gerontology, 195–97
    groupings of older adults, 6, 109, 232
    social gerontology, 91–92, 199
Gilford, Rosalie, 104
Golden Fantasy of marriage, 238
Gottman, John, 101–4
grandchildren
    enjoyment of, 21, 79, 174, 214, 215
    wish for, 80

happiness and well-being
    concern for partner's happiness, 175,
        217
    after divorce, 46–48, 61–64
    enjoyment of children, 21, 36–37, 38,
        59, 153, 174, 215, 217, 227
    enjoyment of grandchildren, 21, 79, 174,
        214, 215
    focus on present moment, 91
    forgiveness, 34, 115
    increased, with age, 13, 88–91, 103, 234
    paradox of aging, 13–14, 88–91

personal happiness ethic, 60
positivity effect, 14, 24, 92, 94–95, 218,
    236
as priority, 16–17
rewarding activities, 75–77, 111
social network and, 22, 199
turnaround of unhappy marriage, 48–51,
    57–60
understanding and renewal, 206–7
U-shaped curve of, 78–79, 218
health concerns
    changes occasioned by, 137–38
    fear of incapacitation, 72
    Medicare for, 144
    mental confusion, 133–38
    as reminders of mortality, 21, 138, 229, 232
    retirement and, 159–62
home mortgage interest deduction, 144
"Hope I Die Before I Get Old" (Lacey), 88
Hymowitz, Kay, 16, 18

Implicit Attitudes Test (IAT), 87–88
Inside the American Couple (Yalom and
    Carstensen), 125–26
Institute for American Values, 61
intermittent reinforcement, 65–67

Johnson, Michael, 52–57

Kalmijn, Matthus, 62–64

Lacey, Heather Pond, 88
later adulthood. See third age
Levenson, Robert, 99, 101–4
Lewis, Myra, 124–25
life expectancy, 1–3, 8–10, 25, 72–73
life span, financial planning throughout,
    195–97
Life-span Development Laboratory (Stanford
    University)
    "Emotional Experience in Everyday Life
        Across the Adult Life Span"
        (Carstensen), 98
    positivity effect study, 94–95
    socioemotional selectivity theory, 93–94
    See also Carstensen, Laura

life-span theory, 104
locus coeruleus, 74, 235
loss of spouse, anticipation of, 29–31,
    197–99

marital endurance ethic, 59–60
marital work ethic, 60
marriage
    abusive relationship, 64–68
    alternatives to, 17–20
    categories of problems, 50–51
    commitment to, 51–57
    Golden Fantasy, 238
    among poor, 19
    trends, 15–17
    turnaround of unhappiness, 48–51,
        57–60
    universal nature of, 16
    See also divorce
Marriage and Caste in America (Hymowitz),
    18
Martin, Steven P., 17–18
Mather, Mara, 95
Medicare, 144
medications
    as cause of sexual problems, 155, 172,
        207, 219, 221
    for sexual problems, 82–83, 128, 129,
        208, 221
menopause, 115–16, 119–22
mental function
    confusion and disorientation, 133–38
    positive changes with aging, 74, 89, 235
    transient global amnesia, 136–38
Mondon, Christiaan W. S., 62–64
money and finance
    arrangements for surviving spouse, 198,
        200, 204–5
    attitudes about, 32–33
    constraints in retirement, 201–5
    cost of children's education, 33–34,
        109–10
    fear of impoverishment, 70, 73
    home mortgage interest deduction, 144
    insufficient savings for retirement,
        190–94, 201–5

management for elderly parents, 72,
    205
Medicare and Social Security benefits,
    144–45
pensions, 141–44
retirement planning, 146–47, 195–97
simplified lifestyle, 110
as source of stress, 31–34, 37, 188–89
moral commitment, 52–54
mortality
    anticipation of spouse's death, 29–31,
        197–99
    awareness of limited time remaining, 14,
        93–94, 104, 138–39, 226–28,
        236
    influence of marriage on, 233
    life expectancy, 1–3, 8–10, 25, 72–73
    longevity in family history, 70, 73
    reminders of, 21, 138, 229, 232

National Incidence Study, 18
National Survey of Families and Households,
    46

older adult couples. *See specific topics*
older adulthood. *See* third age

paradox of aging, 13–14, 88–91
parents
    care of, 71–72, 153–54, 194
    death of, 71, 80, 213, 219, 220,
        224–25
    financial management for, 72, 205
part-time work, 28, 163, 196, 213, 233
pension arrangements, 141–44
personal commitment, 52
personal happiness ethic, 60
physical abuse, 64–68
positivity effect, 14, 24, 92, 94–95, 218,
    236
proactive pruning of social circles, 91–92
Projective Identification, 39

Reiser, Morton, 74, 235
relationships
    emotionally close, 104

influence of family of origin, 37–38, 239

proactive pruning, 91–92

socioemotional selectivity theory, 14, 93–94

transformation of, during "bonus years," 43–44

traumatic bonding, 64–68

unrewarding, elimination of, 91–92, 93, 100–101, 139, 236

well-being and, 22, 199

See also specific topics

retirement

age at, 11, 28, 69, 114, 145–46

creative activities, 111, 147, 151–52, 214, 237

decision, basis for, 11–12

financial concerns, 70, 73, 190–94, 201–5

financial planning for, 195–97

forced, 145–46, 185–86

generativity, 152–53

gradual transition to, 148–51, 162–64, 167–68

health and, 159–62

home mortgage interest deduction, 144

idealized picture of, 199–201

Medicare and Social Security benefits, 144–45

mentoring of younger colleagues, 140, 151, 152

negative views of, 28–29, 145, 159–60, 214

part-time work, 28, 163, 196, 213, 233

pensions, 141–44

positive view of, 146–47

as recent development, 140–41

relocation, 148–50, 168, 199–201

search for meaningful activities, 114–15, 214

volunteer work, 151, 152–53, 163, 214

working wives of retired husbands, 112–13, 190–92

Salovey, Peter, 235

"sandwich generation," 71–72, 153–54, 194

satisfaction. *See* happiness and well-being

Scarf, Maggie, study methods and conclusions, 5–7, 20–24, 26, 166, 233–38

self-esteem

abusive relationships and, 66

divorce and, 47, 53–54

and employment, 12, 145, 160

influence on mortality, 233

and motherhood, 121, 127–28

Sex After Sixty (Butler and Lewis), 124

sexual concerns

female aging, 120–23

frequency of intercourse, 125, 172–74, 207

Internet pornography, 83–86

in loving relationships, 208, 237

low sex drive, 121–23, 126–30, 155–58, 207–9

male aging, 124–25

mastectomy, 221–22

medications, problems caused by, 155, 172, 207, 219, 221

medications for, 82–83, 128, 129, 208, 221

menopause, 119–22

performance anxiety, 82, 124, 127–28

shrinkage of social circle, 14, 91–94

siblings, death of, 71, 80, 205, 212

single motherhood, 18–19

social circle

disapproval of divorce, 55–56, 179

elimination of unrewarding relationships in, 91–92, 93, 100–101, 139, 236

increased activity within, 154

proactive pruning, 91–92

socioemotional selectivity theory, 14, 93–94

well-being and, 22, 199

Social Security benefits, 145

socioemotional selectivity theory (SST), 14, 93–94

spirituality, 23, 107, 205–6
stressors in marriage
    care of elderly parents, 71–72, 153–54,
        194
    children, 50, 57, 78–79, 213, 216–17
    communication and personality
        difficulties, 50–51
    illness, 186–87
    misbehavior of husband, 50
    money, 31–34, 37, 188–89
    multiplicity, 115–16
    resolution of, 48–49, 59, 215
    structural problems outside relationship,
        50, 57–58
structural commitment, 54–57
Suh, Eunkook M., 88

"Taking Time Seriously" (Carstensen and
        Charles), 1, 90–91
third age, 22, 43, 77–78, 117
    concept of "elderly," 4, 237
    cultural messages about, 12–13, 87–88,
        159–60
    as midlife-plus period, 4
    as mirror of adolescence, 11, 25, 42,
        139
    as time for transformation in
        relationship, 43–44
    as young-old years, 6, 139, 232
time remaining
    awareness of, 226–28
    elimination of unrewarding
        relationships, 91–92, 93,
        100–101, 139, 236
    focus on present moment, 91
    horizons throughout life span, 89–91
    life-span theory, 104
    maximizing, 227
    realignment of goals and behavior, 14,
        93–94, 236
    shift in sense of, 138–39
    socioemotional selectivity theory, 14,
        93–94

transient global amnesia (TGA), 136–38, 158
traumatic bonding, 64–68

unhappy marriages
    abuse and traumatic bonding, 64–68
    affection despite, 104
    categories of problems, 50–51
    commitment to, 51–57
    threat of divorce in early years, 20
    turnaround in happiness, 48–51, 57–60
U-shaped curve of marital happiness, 78–79,
        218

Veterans Administration Normative Aging
        Study, 161–62
violence in marriage, 64–68

Waite, Linda J.
    on categories of marital problems, 49–51
    on commitment to unhappy marriages,
        51–52
    happiness after divorce, study of, 45–48,
        61
    on turnaround of unhappy marriages,
        57–60
wealth span cycle, 195–97
well-being. See happiness and well-being
Wilcox, Brad, 18
Williams, Leanne M., 89
withdrawal, emotional, 91–92, 154
work ethic, 160
work ethic, marital, 60
work in retirement
    mentoring, 140, 152
    part-time, 28, 163, 196, 213, 233
    phasing out, 148–51, 162–64, 167–68
    volunteer, 151, 152–53, 163, 214
    working wives of retired husbands,
        112–13, 190–92

Yalom, Marilyn, 125–26
youth, cultural glorification of, 12, 87–88,
        124